FRENCH QUARTER BOUNDARIES AND ORIENTATION

This book takes the boundaries of the French Quarter to be the wide streets at its edges—Canal and Rampart Streets and Esplanade Avenue—and the Mississippi River. It includes both sides of Rampart and Esplanade but only one side of Canal, because the historical position of its median as a "neutral ground" between the Creole and American sectors has implicit within it a strong sense of separation. The official boundaries of the Vieux Carré as a historic district under the jurisdiction of the Vieux Carré Commission are slightly less inclusive.

New Orleans is laid out in successive grids, each tangent at some point to a different curve of the River. The cardinal points are difficult to keep in mind; North and South seem to be constantly shifting. The local solution is to refer to directions as "uptown" or "downtown" based on the flow of the River, uptown meaning upriver, downtown meaning downriver. Directions in the perpendicular direction are based on the River and Lake Pontchartrain. A particular corner of an intersection might be described as "the downtown lake corner," for instance.

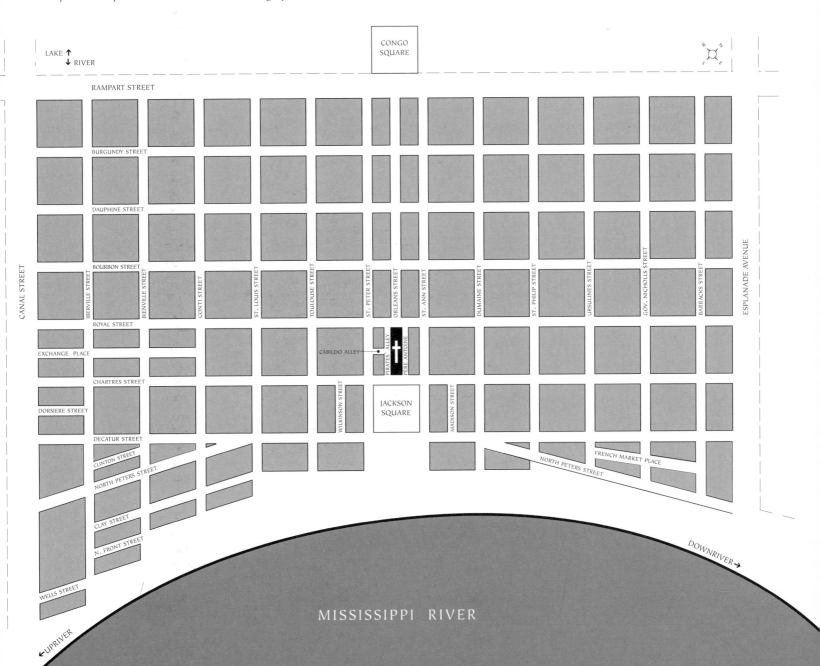

FRENCH QUARTER MANUAL

AN ARCHITECTURAL GUIDE TO NEW ORLEANS' VIEUX CARRÉ

TULANE SCHOOL OF ARCHITECTURE
NEW ORLEANS

FRENCH QUARTER MANUAL

AN ARCHITECTURAL GUIDE TO NEW ORLEANS' VIEUX CARRÉ

MALCOLM HEARD

French Quarter Manual
An Architectural Guide to New Orleans' Vieux Carré
Malcolm Heard

First edition, second printing, 2000

Published by the Tulane School of Architecture
Distributed by the University Press of Mississippi

Designed by Malcolm Heard and Scott Bernhard
Printed in New Orleans by Garrity Printing, Inc.
Set in ITC Tiepolo and Trajan typefaces

Library of Congress Cataloging-in-Publication Data
Heard, Malcolm Whitfield, Jr.
French Quarter Manual, An Architectural Guide to New
Orleans' Vieux Carré/Malcolm Heard
Includes index
ISBN (hardcover) 0-87805-988-1
ISBN (paperback) 0-87805-989-X

Library of Congress Catalog Card Number: 96-72614

Cover Photographs

Front cover: **RH716**
Gardette LePrêtre house,
716 Dauphine Street
1836

Back cover: **RK29**
Napoleon House
500 Chartres Street
1798, 1814

*This book
is dedicated
to*
ALICIANA,
*the place
wherein
it came
about.*

CONTENTS

ACKNOWLEDGMENTS

This book organizes and probes a body of knowledge assembled largely by others. Whatever value it has is built on the foundation of their work.

The first acknowledgement for transmitting a remarkable quantity of that knowledge must go to the late Samuel Wilson, Jr., architect, historian, and teacher. His lifetime of work, continuing that of his partner Richard Koch, provides a resource of enormous value. Mr. Wilson's book *The Vieux Carré, New Orleans, Its Plan, Its Growth, Its Architecture,* recounts the physical history of the French Quarter with documents and maps from an extensive range of sources. Mr. Wilson was instrumental in beginning the Vieux Carré Survey in 1961, along with Professor Bernard Lemann and Dean John Lawrence of the School of Architecture and Boyd Cruise of the Historic New Orleans Collection. The Survey includes a chain of title, architectural evaluation, and accumulated information for each building and site within the French Quarter.

Of special usefulness within the Survey is the succinct architectural description of each property prepared in 1990 by Hilary S. Irvin, Senior Architectural Historian for the Vieux Carré Commission. Ms. Irvin and the Directors and Staff of the Commission and my fellow Commission members were also instructive about the complex workings of the French Quarter community.

The Friends of the Cabildo have established an essential perspective on the architecture and history of the neighborhoods surrounding the Quarter and on Esplanade Avenue in their excellent *New Orleans Architecture* series.

Sally K. Reeves, an author of that series and Archivist of the New Orleans Notarial Archives, took the time to read the text and provide a most helpful collection of comments and recommendations. Ellen Weiss, Professor of Architectural History at Tulane, annotated the text with an inimitable spider web of penciled markings. Full of insight, they were useful in knocking the stilts from beneath various overwrought passages of prose. Whatever stilts remain, and whatever errors, are my own and not those of these readers, nor of Jeannette Hardy, who kindly proofread the text.

Henry Lambert initially suggested this project during his tenure as Director of the Vieux Carré Commission. Teresa Toulouse, my friend and colleague at Tulane, enlarged my perception of the culture behind these buildings.

Gary Van Zante, Curator of the Southeastern Architectural Archive at Tulane, provided direction and logistical help in the selection of photographs. Kevin Williams of the Archive and Joan Caldwell, Curator of the Louisiana Collection, gave valuable assistance. Jan Brantley and Robert Brantley, Alan Karchmer, and Laura Witt provided photographs and willing help.

Frances Hecker, librarian of the Architecture Library at Tulane, was ever resourceful, as were the librarians at the Historic New Orleans Collection. Jon Kukla, Director of the Collection, made photographs of the Collection's structures available.

Friends Betty K. Decell and Eugenie C. Schwarz opened their houses for photographing. Architecture student Rebecca Anderson redrew plans, sections and details for this volume and provided other assistance. Alice Hwang, a recent graduate, contributed a useful study of a French Quarter block.

Architects Eean McNaughton; Robby Cangelosi and Danny Taylor of Koch and Wilson, Architects; Bob Kleinpeter and Chuck Hite of Eskew/Filson Architects; Peter Trapolin and Daniel Samuels of Trapolin Architects; David Waggoner and Charles Sterkx of Waggonner and Ball, Architects; and Creed Brierre supplied photographs, information on twentieth-century restoration projects, and other assistance.

Ann Masson, former Director of Gallier House, was forthcoming with information and help, as were Jan Bradford of the Hermann-Grima House and Professor Jessie Poesch, Professor Emeritus of Art History at Tulane. Tony P. Wrenn, Archivist of the American Institute of Architects in Washington, opened his collection of New Orleans photographs from 1925.

JoAnne Prichard and Richard Abel of the University Press of Mississippi gave time and useful publication advice. Joe Arrigo of Forest Sales was a willing guide through the tricky terrain of book production. Kevin Alker, Paul Garland, and Pat Garrity of Garrity Printing, Inc., collaborated in a multitude of ways in realizing the design of this book. Leslie Myers provided useful explanations of the arcana of computerized layout techniques.

Many forms of support from the Tulane School of Architecture have been essential. The late Dean John Lawrence understood New Orleans as a product, benefactor and victim of time and openly shared his unique vision with me and my generation of students. Important help came from former Deans Ron Filson and Donna Robertson, Acting Dean Don Gatzke, and Professors John Klingman and Eugene Cizek.

My profound gratitude is extended to Bernard Lemann, Professor Emeritus of Architecture at Tulane, an extraordinary teacher in matters of historic preservation, in the layers and complexities of New Orleans culture, and in many other things. His years of stimulating friendship underlie any value this volume may have. His own book, *The Vieux Carré, A General Statement*, portrays the French Quarter with unequalled perception, precision, and grace.

Architect and friend Scott Bernhard has freely collaborated on the design of this book and has cheerfully given more hours of help, support, and useful provocation than I have any possible way to acknowledge.

My children Lucy and Wendell Heard have helped with numerous tasks and in more important ways. My wife, Alicia Rogan Heard, far beyond her work in drawing maps and ironwork for this volume, is the *sine qua non* of the whole enterprise.

New Orleans
March 1997

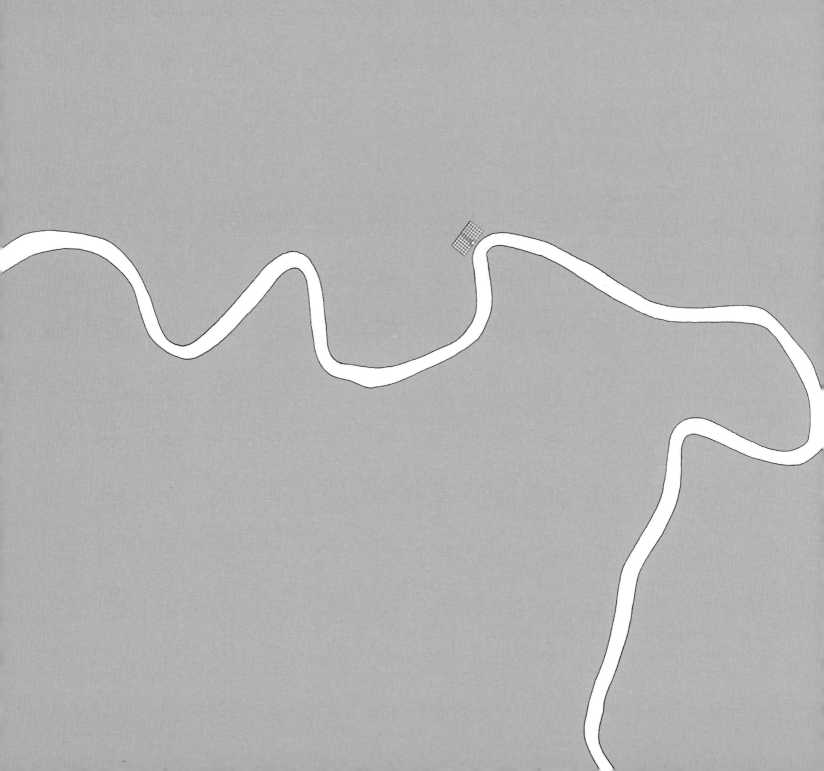

THE GRID ON THE RIVER

THE FRENCH QUARTER GRID

The French Quarter in New Orleans—someone who had never seen it might read descriptions from Faulkner or Walker Percy or Kate Chopin and imagine a Gallic town fragment in a semi-tropical setting. Date palms would outline the curves of its streets as they crossed an undulating ground plane. The earth would slope decisively to the Mississippi River, a langorous presence at the bottom of the scene.

Not so. Gridded as a piece of graph paper and about as flat, the Quarter is actually military in the insistence of its right angles, like the gridded camps Roman soldiers laid out at the wild edges of their empire. Jackson Square sits below high levees holding back the River which at some seasons is higher than the ground itself. The French Quarter looks like what it is—the elaboration of a colonial outpost designed by military engineers.

New Orleans is famously lax in enforcing some forms of civic order. But the street plan of the French Quarter has survived intact from the grid which engineer Adrian de Pauger laid out in 1721. The district contains approximately 100 blocks, most of them squares. Some have been sliced into smaller rectangles, and a few more recent trapezoids adjust to the river's sharp and changing curve. Blocks have been added, more or less symmetrically, at either end of de Pauger's plan. A public square (now Jackson Square) and an *église paroissiale* (now St. Louis Cathedral) sit in the center of the river side, just as he placed them. Behind the Cathedral, Orleans Street still cuts four blocks in half, establishing an axis from the Cathedral Garden to Congo Square, the site of slave gatherings and dances in the nineteenth century.

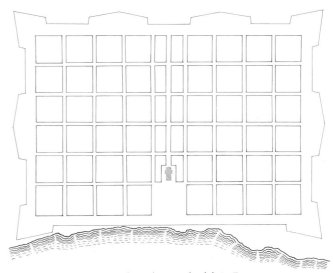

ARH10 plan for New Orleans, 1722, redrawn from Le Blond de La Tour

ARH2 the modern French Quarter

INTRODUCTION

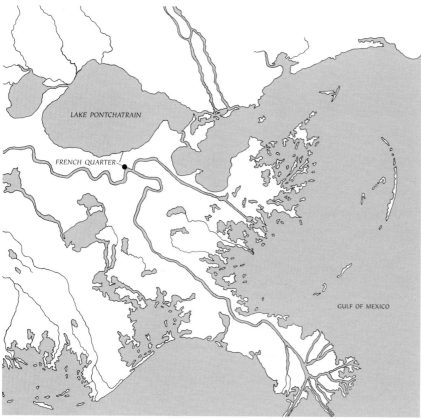

ARH3 Mississippi River delta and Lake Pontchartrain

ARH3 *New Orleans sits on an extreme bend in the Mississippi River, a point where a bayou and a portage connect the River with Lake Pontchartrain.*

RA1 *Early houses sat apart from each other, though many were placed at or near the street. The map suggests the presence of parterred gardens in the spaces around the houses. Whether the geometry of the gardens was real or a refinement of the mapmaker, gardens providing fruit and vegetables would have been vital to the early settlement.*

RA1 Distribution of buildings, 1731, after Gonichon

The street grid is four years younger than the city itself. The founding of New Orleans is dated at the arrival of the Canadian explorer Bienville in 1718. According to a contemporary account he came with six vessels and a few dozen men, many of them convicts.[1] They settled along the riverfront at the foot of the future Conti Street where a loose collection of wood structures was set about in a clearing cut from canebrake. The narrow path of an Indian portage connected them with Bayou St. John, which meandered to Lake Pontchartrain and gave the future city a "back door" to the Gulf of Mexico. This rear entrance, offering vessels an alternative to navigating the ninety miles of dangerous river between New Orleans and the Gulf, was the determining factor in placing the new settlement.[2] Surrounded by swamps and susceptible to flooding, the location had little else to recommend it.

In 1721 the French proposed a more orderly fortified town. Engineer Le Blond de la Tour drew the plan for it while living at Biloxi, the French settlement to the east on the Gulf of Mexico. De Pauger, his assistant, came to New Orleans and laid the plan out. A regular town grid was imposed with force over the original makeshift arrangement of buildings. One account tells of a man imprisoned and beaten nearly to the point of blindness for protesting the destruction of his own house, positioned unhappily in the middle of one of the new grid's streets. De la Tour's original Place d'Armes is the focus of an orthogonal network of streets named, as they still are, to honor Louis XV, the Regent (Philip, Duke of Orleans) and other members of the French court.

New Orleans began, not inappropriately some would say, as a well-intended speculation. John Law, Scottish monetary reformer who became comptroller general of France, financed the settlement through his Company of the West. He attracted French investors with broadsides touting the colony's real and imagined riches. When Law's company went bankrupt in 1720, the resulting financial debacle became known as the Mississippi Bubble. (From that perspective New Orleans' more recent experience with a bankrupt casino at the Quarter's edge seems no more than one of many replays of the initial speculation of its founding.)

John Chase's lively history of the city's streets points out the role of the street names in lending credibility to Law's enterprise and flattering the Regent and the King whose support was critical.[3] The prefix St. was placed before the names of these men (St. Philip Street for the Regent, St. Louis Street for the young Louis XV), creating a useful ambiguity between temporal and spiritual authority. Similarly, naming the church at the Place d'Armes for St. Louis reasserted the divine source of the current young king's right to rule at the same time it honored Louis IX, the saint.

The Frenchmen who made the new town plan were trained in the principles of military engineering. Before New Orleans, they had drawn a plan for the settlement on the Gulf of Mexico at Biloxi. It showed a simple grid set within an intricate geometric pattern of fortifications, suggesting great battlements in a pattern of interlocking stars. Such fortifications were in the spirit of the work of Vauban, military engineer for Louis XIV, and they continued to surround the drawings of the New Orleans grid when the engineers moved their attention from Biloxi to the new settlement on the Mississippi River. No fortifications of the kind were ever built of course, a fact which reveals a telling disparity between the engineers' vision and the true nature of John Law's

Mississippi Bubble. Defense of the colony and the colonists was never so important as dreams of economic prosperity. Settlers came, however, and they survived and built. Their buildings were straightforward, but they expressed from the beginning a certain particularity of place which has continued to mark their successors.

The first houses sat apart from each other, on sites made of combinations or divisions of the twelve original lots in each typical block (p. 9). Early maps show many houses placed flush with the street line, and the first landowners were required as a condition of ownership to erect palisades at the street (map, p. 2). From earliest times there was some sense of wall along the street edges, a condition that survives today. Productive gardens growing fruits and vegetables were important to the residents. Early maps are spotted with them, generally laid out in symmetrical patterns with paths between the beds. Madame John's Legacy (pp. 18, 118) is the surviving house in the Quarter—it feels like an early plantation house—where it is easiest to imagine the French Colonial town, though it sits on only a portion of its original site.

The denser, more urban French Quarter ground plan we know today, common-wall structures and detached cottages intermingled with courtyards, began to emerge in the Spanish Colonial period (1763-1803). When Spain officially acquired New Orleans and all the French territory west of the Mississippi, New Orleans was a town of perhaps 5,000. It wasn't until 1769 that the Spanish forcefully asserted their authority with the arrival of the Spanish-Irish General Alexandro O'Reilly. Once asserted, Spanish authority was relatively benign, and Gallic traditions persisted under Spanish governors.

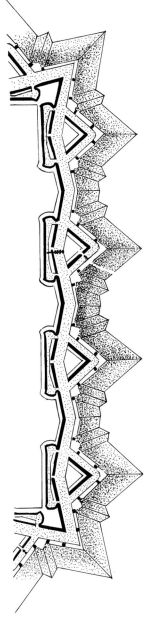

ARH14 *Fortifications shown on Pierre Baron's map of 1729 are the basis for this drawing. Such fortifications decorated many maps of New Orleans, but nothing so magnificent ever came close to being built.*

3

K34 707-09 Dumaine Street, c. 1799 (see also p. 13)

K34 *Built a few years after the new fire-prevention ordinances went into effect, this surviving Spanish Colonial cottage has the required flat roof. It also followed the requirement for stuccoed masonry construction, though as a one-story building it was legally exempt.*

Spanish cultural influence took physical form after the disastrous fires of 1788 and 1794 destroyed most of the early colonial structures. According to Spanish Governor Miro, 850 structures were burned in 1788 alone. Thinking to avoid future conflagrations, the Spanish Cabildo in 1795 passed laws which limited the use of wood and wood shingles in new houses. The new regulations required that houses of more than one story be built of brick or brick-between-posts, plastered over, a common construction method since early French days. Roofs had to be flat (or relatively so) and built of tile or brick, a dramatic change from the steep roof pitches favored by the French. As such structures proliferated, the physical character of the Quarter evolved accordingly—the influence of northern French building traditions, transmitted to some degree through the cold Canadian provinces, waned in favor of the more Mediterranean forms of the Spanish. Contiguous buildings with plastered surfaces came to form the walls of many streets. In the older parts of the Quarter today, mottled, tinted stucco becomes almost continuous as one building and its courtyard walls lean against the next. But through all these constructions and reconstructions, the original gridded plan held firm.

Early maps for some years show an anomaly within the grid—a road angling off to Bayou St. John, following the path of the ancient Indian portage. Late in the Spanish period a new linear element appears on maps. Governor Carondelet began construction in 1792 of a canal which connected Bayou St. John with the rear of the old city near the point where St. Peter and Basin Streets intersect today. The canal's turning basin gave the name to Basin Street, not a French Quarter street but intimately related to its history. The Carondelet (or Old Basin) Canal brought ships from local and foreign ports to the city's back door. Surviving until 1927, the canal accounts for the unexpected appearance of masts and sails in nineteenth drawings of the Rampart Street area.

In the 1790s Governor Carondelet had also constructed five forts around the town with palisades and moats between them. By the time of the Louisiana Purchase little remained of these limited fortifications but the forts themselves. They survived for a few more years, rendered useless by rotten palisades and half-filled moats.[4]

After the Louisiana Purchase in 1803, the United States found itself in possession of a city of 7,000 inhabitants and a foreign building tradition.[5] American building preferences led gradually to the construction of substantial exposed brick stuctures, some detached, many contiguous with their neighbors. The American exposed brick townhouse of 1835 would have had an enclosed hallway, while his Creole neighbor built, at the same date, a plastered brick house with an open carriageway. But the pattern of structures, built tight to the street and embracing an interior courtyard, persisted.

The population grew dramatically after the Louisiana Purchase, reaching 24,000 by 1810, 46,000 by 1830, and 116,375 by 1850.[6] Variations in the street grid were few but had their impact. Le Blond de la Tour's original six-block-by-nine-block rectangle elongated somewhat, to Canal Street upriver and to Esplanade Avenue downriver. Canal and Rampart Streets and Esplanade Avenue all occupy space where the fortifications had been. A clue that Esplanade was not one of the original streets of the military engineers is the row of non-square, narrow blocks separating it from Barracks Street. Some property lines within these blocks, as well as on the Canal Street end, still reflect the diagonal direction of the old fortifications.

The intrepid Ursuline nuns, an important civilizing influence in the raw French outpost of the 1720s, had enclosed a portion of the grid for a hundred years. Closing first one and then two blocks of Chartres street, they consolidated a four-block parcel bounded by Ursulines, Barracks, Decatur and Royal Streets. In addition to their convent, these blocks contained a hospital and the military barracks for the colony. This parcel remained closed off from the street grid until about 1820 when the nuns moved to their new convent downriver and the city reopened the streets.

One-block-long streets were cut through three of the Quarter's existing blocks. Dorsière Street, connecting Iberville to Canal, provided an additional link with the developing American sector, the Faubourg St. Mary. In the two blocks on either side of Jackson Square, Wilkinson and Madison Streets were opened in 1816 and 1826, respectively. Both streets cut land that had been publicly owned, allowing a coherent layout of accessible lots within the blocks.

The impulse to open the Quarter toward the American sector stimulated the development of Exchange Place, intended as an incision from Canal Street to the heart of the Quarter. American developers proposed the project of the 1830s, together with a plan for continuous arcaded façades. The plan was to slice the blocks between Royal and Chartres Streets, extending the new street six blocks from Canal to the side of the Cathedral. Its course would have included the lobby of the St. Louis Hotel, which with its slave ex-

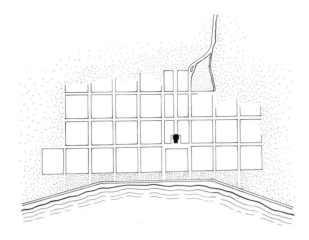

ARH4 town and portage, 1728, from Gonichon

ARH4 *By 1728 this portion of the projected town plan had been developed. The portage road in the upper right connected Bayou St. John with St. Ann and Dumaine Streets. It may originally have extended diagonally to meet the River near the foot of Conti Street, the location of the settlers' first clearing.*

ARH7 *The diagonal line of old fortifications is still discernible in property lines and even building shapes in blocks at the ends of the Quarter.*

ARH5 *Governor Carondelet's canal connected the rear of the French Quarter with Bayou St. John and Lake Pontchartrain. It parallels the less direct line of the old portage.*

ARH7 layout of a block fronting on Esplanade Avenue

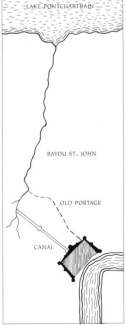

ARH5 Carondelet Canal

5

INTRODUCTION

M8 Exchange Place seen from now-demolished block

M8 *Exchange Place bisected four blocks from Canal Street to St. Louis in the 1830s. This photograph was taken from the fourth block, some time before 1907-09 when the Civil Courts Building was constructed. The Courts Building closed the street and replaced a significant number of eighteenth-and nineteenth-century structures.*

ARH6 *The blocks shown in black occupy the wedge of land added to the French Quarter by the shifting path of the River during the nineteenth century.*

ARH6 Blocks added to the French Quarter after 1818

change and related commerical enterprises was a commercial hub. Four block lengths plus a separate fraction now known as Cabildo Alley were actually built, but one block was eliminated in the early twentieth century when an entire original square was demolished for construction of the Civil Courts Building at 400 Royal Street.

The Mississippi River is responsible for a sizeable addition to the French Quarter grid. Both the reason New Orleans was founded and the city's nemesis, the River plies a tortuous path past the city to the Gulf of Mexico, carrying strong and fickle currents and demonstrating no regard for the rational grid of the French engineers. Its annual threats to innundate New Orleans are countered by an elaborately built and maintained system of levees. In a cooperative gesture during the nineteenth century, however, it shifted its course at the particularly sharp curve where the French Quarter is located and deposited a wedge of land just upriver from Jackson Square. The new land shows up dramatically in comparing a map of 1818 with Robinson's Atlas of 1873.[7] Four blocks wide and several hundred feet in depth, the new land came along at the same time the city's commerce was thriving. The wharves moved out onto land that had been river, and several new streets became the location of sheds, railroad tracks, and structures for Louisiana's flourishing sugar industry. Rows of railroad tracks threaded their way through the area, serving the wharfs and bringing passengers to the foot of Canal Street.

In the 1960s a plan emerged to construct a riverfront expressway through this area, separating the French Quarter from the river. The scheme, originally proposed by planner Robert Moses in 1946 had enormous support, and only the most determined efforts of local preservationists, aided at the last moment by the President's Advisory Council on Historic Preservation, prevented the disaster.[8]

Along the River today, most of the warehouse and wharf structures are gone, along with several of the nineteenth century streets. On the riverfront are the Moonwalk from the 1970s, and Woldenberg Park and the Aquarium of the Americas built in the 1980s atop the levees and outside the Army Corps of Engineers' floodwall. The landscaped margin of Woldenberg Park is suspended above the river on piles, a strange site from the River, but a popular waterside prom-enade, replacing the barrier of the old wharf sheds. Planners of the Park and the Aquarium made efforts to extend the Quarter's transverse streets into the riverfront area, though not to the water's edge. Behind the park, on the Quarter side of the Canal Place shopping center and hotel development, sits land strangely empty and used for parking lots. Tourism, the city's economic motor in the late twentieth cen-tury, will probably determine what goes in this space, just as the sugar industry did in the last century. That the streets and build-ings of this newest part of the Quarter be as well-made and agreeably scaled as their older neighbors is the intention of the Quarter's partisans, a wish never expressed without trepidation. If thoughtful planning of the area is sacrificed to short term gain and political expediency, the loss of opportunity will be enormous. Exemplified by the ex-pressway proposal, the forces of twentieth century change have been notoriously heavy-handed.

FRENCH QUARTER SPACE

An architectural riddle: if the French Quarter works as an urban environment, which of its aspects is most essential? A strong case can be made for space.

Most of the buildings are hardly perceivable as objects because they cannot be seen in the round. Rather they serve as shapers of space—of the rooms and courtyards within them and of the streets which they confine. The town blocks and their buildings can be imagined as solids that have been eaten away, like old furniture full of worm holes. There is energy in these erosions; they are full of intent. The energy lies in the tension between the clear street grid and the idio-syncratic spaces stacked and wedged and hung in interstices behind the streets. Within the thousands of spaces and in the se-quences between them reside what might be called the Quarter's myths, myths in the plural because, like the buildings themselves, they have been built up in layers over time, with much lost along the way. George Schmidt, exceptional both as a painter of New Orleans and as its observer and critic, identifies the Quarter's layers of myth with those who have written of it—one thinks of George Washington Cable, Kate Chopin, William Faulkner, Tennessee Williams, Walker Percy, John Kennedy Toole. Each has defined a particular French Quarter which is alive in books and plays and in the minds of people who read the books and see the plays. Readers who live in the Quarter can bring the myths to the place where they live and cause them to seep into the physical place. Myths intensify themselves. Because courtyards have been described as tropical or jungle-like, people plant more banana trees and palms.

INTRODUCTION

MW123 The name of Madame John's Legacy preserves a fictional situation imagined by George Washington Cable. Paradoxically the fiction has become a layer of the house's reality.

Madame John's Legacy, one of the Quarter's landmarks, is so named not because any living woman named Madame John ever inherited it, but because George Washington Cable wrote a charming story in which she did; he indentified the house convincingly, linked the fictional character to it, and the name has stuck. The world of Cable's story has been attached to the house, and the house is richer for it. A book such as this *Manual*, principally analytical,

shows only part of a picture, an intellectualized taxonomy of pieces. But it is obliged to acknowledge the other realm of the associational, the experiential. Many of the photographs printed in this book are selected to that end—views framed by a particular photographer's eye at a particular moment which may have the power to extend our way of seeing beyond our own time and our favorite intellectual categories.

MW123 Madame John's Legacy, 628-32 Dumaine Street, 1788

THE FRENCH QUARTER BLOCK

The French Quarter block is a square about 320 feet on a side (300 seventeenth-century French feet). Initially each block was divided into twelve lots. The modern property lines of any block reflect nearly two centuries of subdivisions, recombinations and shifted boundaries—a block plan is a line drawing decipherable as an intricate history of ambi-tions, hard times, family alliances, disputes between neighbors. Even so, the ghost of the original twelve lots is often discernible. Seeing a square from above, a labyrinth of passages and courtyards opens it to light and air. Passing by on the street, one looks through the darkness of tunnel-like carriageways into the green middles of blocks. Beyond the arrow-straight streets, behind the façades, there is irregularity, surprise and a measure of mystery.

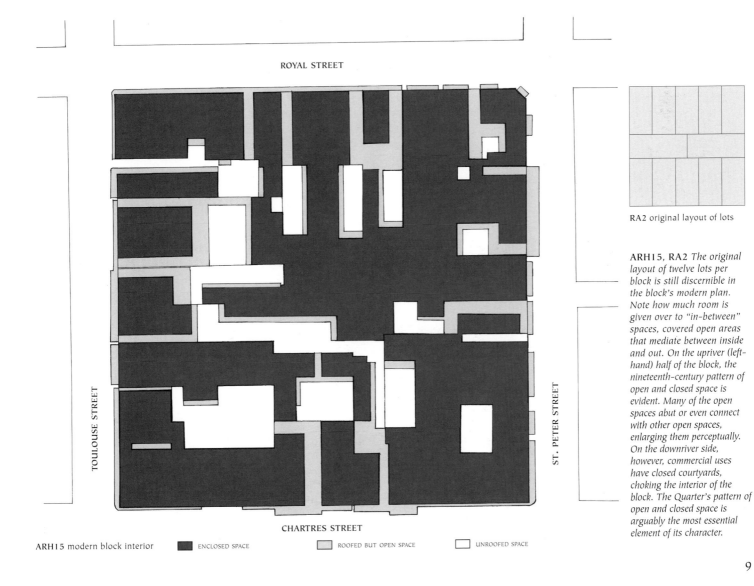

ROYAL STREET

TOULOUSE STREET

ST. PETER STREET

CHARTRES STREET

RA2 original layout of lots

ARH15, RA2 *The original layout of twelve lots per block is still discernible in the block's modern plan. Note how much room is given over to "in-between" spaces, covered open areas that mediate between inside and out. On the upriver (left-hand) half of the block, the nineteenth-century pattern of open and closed space is evident. Many of the open spaces abut or even connect with other open spaces, enlarging them perceptually. On the downriver side, however, commercial uses have closed courtyards, choking the interior of the block. The Quarter's pattern of open and closed space is arguably the most essential element of its character.*

ARH15 modern block interior   ■ ENCLOSED SPACE   ▪ ROOFED BUT OPEN SPACE   □ UNROOFED SPACE

INTRODUCTION

K186 700 Royal Street, detail

Early records refer to the blocks in French as *îles*, not literally meaning islands, but a suggestive term when frequent rains and floods and difficult drainage conditions turned streets into canals. Straining the metaphor (beyond discreet limits, perhaps) the sidewalk occurred on the "bank", and is still occasionally called the banquette (pronounced BANK-et) in local usage.

THE FRENCH QUARTER STREET

But the streets—they remain as rectangular volumes of space grown up from the French engineers' grid, their walls roughly as high as their width. The average width of the original streets is 22 feet, curb to curb, plus an eight-foot sidewalk on each side. Orleans Street, in its central position, is seven feet wider. In this system, intersections of streets become Cartesian coordinates for identifying locations. Consistent and orderly, the streets are a rational foil to the architectural and social non-conformity evident both on the streets and behind the walls that enclose them. Each of the types of buildings constructed along the Quarter's streets—the Creole cottage, the town house, the shotgun, even many of the early French Colonial houses—planted itself squarely on the street property line, giving shape and an edge to the street, channeling movement within its spatial volume. Variations in the street's wall, the occasional setback, the more frequent courtyard wall with sometimes a tree hanging over it, change the street volume's height as they intensify or soften its sense of enclosure.

An essential component of the modern French Quarter street appeared after 1850 when the Pontalba Buildings introduced the large-scale use of cast iron to the district. Two and three-story galleries proliferated, covering the entire widths of sidewalks. Their room-like volumes, outlined with dense cast iron vines, heavy with sculpted flowers and fruits, often replaced narrower balconies of restrained, geometric wrought iron. A new vertical layer of filigree and air—elevated, stacked, spacious outdoor cages—extended over the sidewalks to the very curbs of the streets. The upstairs rooms within the buildings, usually residential, opened to the new galleries through casement doors and cleverly designed window sashes, high enough to allow people to move out easily. Galleries became at once sitting rooms, viewing platforms, and side stages—integral to the street theater below.

With their controlled shape and projecting iron-framed volumes, the streets of the French Quarter and of all New Orleans, are more than a path for movement; they are places in themselves, scenes for a pageant. More than any building, they have provided the setting what are surely the city's essential art forms—the early jazz music of the marching bands and the parades of Mardi Gras. The character of the streets makes them at once orderly and inviting to music and parades and carnival. Buildings provide the backdrop, iron galleries the wings, and changing weather the lighting and special effects. Ordinary people become performers.

FRENCH QUARTER BUILDINGS

The buildings that form the walls of French Quarter streets will not be found in architecture textbooks; they are not great architecture in that sense. Most are simple products of what is now referred to as the vernacular architecture of their time. Yet as one comes to know them, these plain self-assured structures reveal admirable amounts of cleverness and rectitude and sometimes a gratuitous beauty that takes one by surprise.

RH700 700 Royal Street, the Labranche buildings

K52 700 Royal Street, the Labranche buildings

K186, RH700, K52
Galleries bounded by ironwork, all added decades after construction, round the Royal Street corner of the Labranche buildings, shown from three different positions. Galleries are claimed by the building but are also part of the street, projecting over the public sidewalk. They mediate between building and street, making the relationship more complex and interactive.

INTRODUCTION

K105 600 block of Bourbon Street

K105, K12 *One of the rhythms of the French Quarter Street comes from juxtapositions of scales. Creole cottages sit without apology next to three-story town houses. Jumping building heights, obvious in these photographs, are less apparent to the pedestrian, who notices principally the continuity of walls at eye level.*

K12 address uncertain

Most of this book is about these buildings, cataloging and defining the basic building types into which they fit, the architectural styles that have dressed them, and a set of components common to most of them. The decision to organize the book by both *type* and *style* is fundamental to its approach, as explained on page 15. The components section is a kit of parts, illustrating familiar elements such as windows, transoms and shutters which occur on all types and styles of buildings and at all scales. Components can be seen as a kind of sub-set of the types, conventional elements repeated from building to building with infinite variation. Components may appear in several types of buildings and are subject to mutations brought on by changing styles.

The *scale* of buildings is something architects love to discuss, and its role in French Quarter buildings is fundamental. Scale refers to relative size, the size of one building compared to another or of one part of a building compared to another part. Scale has much to do with whether a building is grand or modest. It is great fun to watch how scale and type and style interact on a French Quarter street. A Greek Revival town house can be almost self-effacing if its windows and doors and rooms are small and its neighbors are large. The simple Creole cottage can become an impressive dwelling when its ceilings are thirteen feet tall and its transoms have the delicately-curving muntins of the Federal style. Varieties of scale and the refinement of style in these buildings mirror the self-images and the aspirations of the people who built and have inhabited them. For most of its history (with the present day one of the exceptions) the Quarter has been home to a striking cross section of the city's population. The juxtaposition of rich and poor has led here (as through-

MW121 707-09 Dumaine Street. c. 1799

out New Orleans) to the most amazing architectural juxtapositions, part and parcel of the concomitant human interactions.

The buildings shown here are selected to serve the book's specific organization and to illustrate the richness of the Quarter's architectural inventory. Many more good buildings and many public and private spaces are missing from these pages. Another book needs to catalog and illustrate several hundred of these—some which exemplify the types and styles outlined here and others which reveal the limits of these taxonomies by not fitting anywhere. When juxtaposition is where the energy lies, variety is everything. Categories are hard-pressed to keep up.

MW121 *In the categories of this book, this building is a flat-roofed Spanish Colonial cottage. But striped with chevrons as a "shaving-parlor", it shouts the bloodless nature, or at least the limitations, of such categories.*

13

BY TYPE OR BY STYLE?

This book shows two ways of "reading" the French Quarter's buildings. One is to divide them into *types* of buildings based on size and shape—cottages, town houses, shotguns, etc. The other is to divide them into recognizable *styles* of design—French colonial, Greek revival, etc.—that correspond with certain dates and sometimes with recognized categories of architectural style found in buildings in other parts of the world at roughly the same time. These two approaches are often confused; people will speak of a Creole cottage or a shotgun house as a *style* of building, when actually they represent a certain arrangement of mass and space which were, at different times, dressed in a number of different styles.

Many buildings cross over between clear categories of type and style; they are hybrid in some way. The Gallier House (p. 47) has characteristics of both the Creole and the American townhouse. In other cases later alterations obscure the categories—Creole cottages, for example, were remodeled to look like double shotguns. Sometimes these changes detract from the original structure, other times they improve its adaptation to changing conditions. The Vieux Carré's pioneer preservation legislation of 1936 recognized this complexity. It set out with admirable foresight to preserve the value of what it calls the Quarter's "quaint and distinctive character." A 1941 court case defined the inclusiveness of the preservationist mandate, using the term *tout ensemble*—embracing buildings, *and* their changes over time, *and* their context of streets and other open spaces. A useful contrast is often made between the French Quarter and Colonial Williamsburg. Whereas Williamsburg preserves and reconstructs a specific eighteenth-century environment, the Quarter is a chronicle of change over time, a palimpsest showing how a living community came to be the way it is—and how it continues to change.

MH90 *At first glance these two façades appear to be the fronts of double shotgun houses. They are decorated with the door frames, brackets, soffit ventilators and other machine-made detail typically found on the shotgun type. But a look at the shapes of the houses—given away by the direction of the roof ridges—reveals them to be Creole cottages which were "modernized" some half century after construction. A style has been applied to a type, making it appear to be another type.*

MH90 821-23, 827-29 St. Peter Street, both cottages c. 1830, remodeled in the late nineteenth century

15

TYPES OF FRENCH QUARTER HOUSES

RECOGNIZING TYPES OF BUILDINGS

The façade of the St. Louis Cathedral looks like a stage set. On clear days the sun rises from stage left and keeps the façade illuminated most of the day. Facing southeast a little stiffly, the Cathedral confronts another prop, the sculpture of Andrew Jackson on his rearing horse in silhouette against the backdrop of Decatur Street and the levee. The top of the levee becomes an elevated horizon above which the stacks of ships glide artificially, like cut-out images propelled by hidden hands.

The Cathedral presides over a collection of French Quarter buildings, most of which are residential or partly residential. The co-existence within a single building of residential and commercial uses is a principal characteristic of French Quarter land use. This mixed usage of property provides a model for a lively and civilized urbanity much sought after by designers of modern communities.

Most of the surviving buildings date from the nineteenth century. There is also a generous scattering of eighteenth- and twentieth-century structures. The eighteenth-century ones are prized for their scarcity; fires in 1788 and 1794 burned nearly everything. The twentieth-century buildings are not yet prized but will come to be, representing a lively if inchoate diversity characteristic of their (our) time.

Among the surviving buildings are a few churches and public structures, all of individual architectural interest, but not the main concern of this study of *types*. Its principal subject is the residential buildings, including service structures and often ground-floor stores, which comprise most of the Quarter's building stock. It is these buildings that establish the Quarter's architectural matrix. The few basic types they represent were repeated over and over with rich variations. At their best they demonstrate the subtle refinement possible when a circumscribed form of building receives the grace of human attention over a period of decades.

Most buildings in the French Quarter fall into five basic types that are easy to recognize by their size and shape:

THE FRENCH COLONIAL HOUSE,
THE SPANISH COLONIAL HOUSE,
THE COTTAGE,
THE TOWN HOUSE,
THE SHOTGUN HOUSE.

RH800 *This corner Creole town house with its courtyard wall and three-story service structure displays a tall profile to Dumaine Street. Arched loggia openings overlook the courtyard from the second floor. Painted signs and streetcar tracks and wires syncopate photographer Rudolf Hertzberg's image. Of the signs shown, only the Uneeda Biscuit advertisement in the distance has survived time and the current sign ordinance.*

TYPES

M10 Madame John's Legacy, or the Manuel Lanzos house, 628-32 Dumaine Street, 1788

FRENCH COLONIAL HOUSE
DATES: BUILT FROM 1718 TO THE 1780s

No house is known to survive in New Orleans from the French Colonial period; time and the disastrous fires of the late eighteenth century took them away. The only surviving whole structure (there are undoubtedly fragments here and there) is the Ursuline Convent of 1745-1750. Together with some early maps and records, we have the Convent to give us some sense of the buildings the French Colonists put up. In addition there is one house from 1788, a date well into the Spanish period, that provides a near copy of the kind of French Colonial house it replaced. Madame John's Legacy (628 Dumaine Street) looks to us more like a plantation house than a town house. It supplies a revealing view of eighteenth-century New Orleans and an example of a once-common house type.

The similarity to early plantation houses is not accidental. Like them, Madame John's sat free-standing on its site, an irregular lot some 84 feet wide by just under 120 feet deep. Early maps and drawings imply a prevalence of such establishments, drawn as rectangles among geometrical beds of planting and scattered outbuildings, surroundings similar to those of plantation houses of the period. Samuel Wilson, Jr., authority on the buildings of New Orleans and the region, observed that the size of the house on the Gonichon map of 1731 (see p. 2) corresponds with the present house without its galleries.[1] (*Gallery* in local usage is a general term for porch.) In contrast to its immediate predecessor on this site, possibly the house on the 1731 map, Madame John's was positioned close to the street and on a smaller lot (the town was becoming denser) and, significantly, had galleries, front and back. Without the tall ground floor, the galleries and their roofs—

M10, Madame John's Legacy sits squarely on the sidewalk, its main floor raised. Goods were stored on the ground level. It is thought to be a near copy of the French Colonial house which preceded it on this site. The earlier house was set back from the street on a larger lot.

RA3 Both stairways to the main level are external, one on each gallery. Openings from rooms to the galleries are arranged according to the requirements of function and the interior geometry, with no effort made to align them between the gallery columns. Outbuildings on the irregular lot include a kitchen with cook's quarters and another two-story service structure.

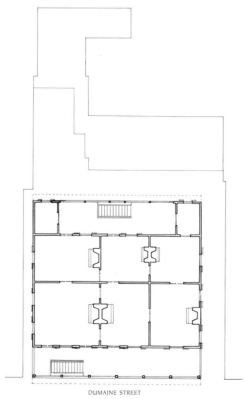

DUMAINE STREET

RA3 Madame John's Legacy, main floor plan

without, that is, the adaptations made to the wetness and heat—the similarities with the Ursuline Convent would be striking. There is the same steep roof spread over a truss, the same casement windows and doors with segmental arches, the same batten shutters.

The presence of galleries on such a building was a major architectural innovation. Assumed to be of Caribbean inspiration, galleries adapted the severe forms of French Canada to the hot sun and heavy rainfall of New Orleans. The appendage of galleries gave open-air living and sleeping space to houses while shading their openings from sun and allowing them to remain open during rains. First attached as shallow-roofed additions galleries, by 1750 at least, were incorporated into the design of new structures. The makeshift roof line of an added porch was gradually smoothed into the familiar double-pitched roof found in town and country houses throughout the area. *See "Roofs" under Construction, p.148.* The galleries show a fundamental aspect of the local architectural tradition, the development of a wide range of incremental degrees of "outsideness". On Madame John's there are two kinds of galler-ies—the front one open on three sides, the rear one enclosed on three sides.

Raised some eight feet, the main level is a series of interconnected rooms and galleries of various sizes. The walls of this raised level are of brick between posts rather than the thicker solid brick of the ground floor. Raising the house not only eased the problem of flooding at a time when weak levees were an uncertain defense against rising water but also lifted the living areas to a breezier elevation. The upper exterior walls are covered with wide beaded weatherboards. The front gallery extends the full width of the front and the rear one is inset between two *cabinets* (see p.114). It is on these

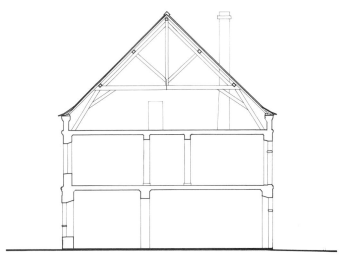

RA4 Ursuline Convent, transverse section

RA5 Madame John's Legacy, transverse section

RA4, RA5 *Trusses in French Colonial buildings evolved to accommodate galleries. The slope of the central part of the truss of Madame John's Legacy is similar to that of the Ursuline Convent. But Madame John's has a king post (the central vertical member), a lower tie beam (the horizontal member), and important additional rafters extending out at a shallower pitch. These rafters transform the roof slope to a double pitch which extends protection to the galleries on both sides. In good weather the usable space of the house extends to the galleries' edges. During rain the gallery roofs allow doors and windows to remain open. In cold weather the house contracts to a more easily heated volume. The space of the attic remains tall but expands horizontally.*

19

TYPES

K9, MH82 *This house has the casements, segmentally-arched openings, and brick-between-posts construction of French Colonial buildings. It is one of the Quarter's oldest houses. Research by the Orleans Parish Landmarks Commision indicates it was built on this site in 1780, the parts having been dismantled from a still earlier house on Bayou St. John. It is another example of the continuation of French Colonial building practices into the Spanish Colonial period. The brick-between-posts construction was originally covered, but at some time in the decades since the earlier picture was taken the wood sheathing was stripped from the façade. Such exposure of fragile old timber and masonry to the elements leaves them without the protection they were intended to have. It is poor preservation practice.*

K9 Gabriel Peyroux house, 901-07 Burgundy Street, 1780

MH82 Peyroux house photographed in 1997

A British engineer, Captain Philip Pittman, described New Orleans in an account published in London in 1770.

The general plan of building in the town, is with timber frames filled up with brick; and most of the houses are built of one floor, raised about eight feet from the ground, with large galleries round them, and the cellars under the floors, level with the ground; it is impossible to have any subterraneous buildings, as they would be constantly full of water. I imagine that there are betwixt seven and eight hundred houses in the town, most of which have gardens. The squares at the back and sides of the town are mostly laid out in gardens; the orange trees, with which they are planted, are not unpleasant objects, and in the spring afford an agreeable smell.

The Present State of the European Settlements
on the Mississippi, London, 1770[2]

exterior galleries that stairs rise from the ground. The front windows and doors do not line up between the turned wood columns; such a lack of alignment is as characteristic of plantation houses of this period as the double-pitched hipped roof. Its shape sheds water on all four sides, another expression that the house was built not as an urban town house, but with space all around it.

The wide interior floor boards are made of cypress, as are the ceilings and joists, conversions of ancient swamp timber to the materials of shelter. The thin, paneled double doors have iron hardware. There are simple wooden mantels wrapping three sides of the chimneys, the substantial bases of which hunker in the ground level space. The unfinished attic is dominated by the pegged beams and trusses supporting the complex sculpture of the double-pitched, hipped roof. Once probably shingled in wood, it is now slated. The small dormers are thought to have been added around 1820, contemporary with the turned posts on the front gallery; originally these supports were chamfered posts like those on the rear.

Madame John's Legacy would not have been considered a small house. It was built for a captain of the Spanish regiment and later housed other prominent citizens. Variants of this kind of house must have been common in New Orleans and in the country during the eighteenth century, a response to local needs, synthesized from French and French Colonial precedents (including Canadian ones) and from West Indian building practices. Seeing these houses as an evolution within only one tradition seems wrong, given the lively cultural mix from which they grew. If the triangular trusses bearing on the major walls look clearly French, the raised nature of the house and the extensions of rafters to cover galleries seem as clearly derived from West Indian buildings.

SPANISH COLONIAL HOUSE
DATES: BUILT AFTER 1763 TO THE EARLY 1800s

Conventional wisdom has it that the Spanish introduced the courtyard to New Orleans. That is not a bad way of framing the changes in French Quarter houses that came about during the forty years of the Spanish Colonial period. The French Colonial house had sat with ample room around it, and the only areas resembling a courtyard were the residual spaces between principal and service structures. But inside Spanish Colonial houses, one gets the sense of a courtyard as an intentional, perhaps even a designed space, not simply an absence of building. The courtyard becomes room-like in its enclosure and dimensions.

The Spanish Colonial courtyard is normally reached not by walking around the house as at Madame John's, but by entering a carriageway cut through the volume of the building. At the end of the carriageway is another covered space, a loggia, which is open to the courtyard through breaks, often arches, in a thick stuccoed brick wall. The loggia contains the stairway to the upper, residential part of the house, leaving the front rooms at street level for commercial use or the exercise of a trade. Behind is some configuration of kitchen and service rooms. Sometimes these are positioned as an ell; sometimes they are a separate structure.

If this begins to sound very much like the description of the Creole town house, (p. 38), that is because the Creole town house is a regularized version of the Spanish Colonial house. The Spanish Colonial house is distinguished precisely by its lack of regularization; each surviving example is different from the others. What is new about them, and

M3 Bosque house, 617-19 Chartres Street, 1795

M3 The loggia is at left in this corner of the Bosque house courtyard. The large arch is aligned with the carriageway from the street. Elliptical arches with casements and fanlights give a degree of enclosure to the upper level of the loggia. The lower-ceilinged service structure begins at the wooden balcony. Wood railings (the particular design shown is probably a later alteration) were commonly used not only on service structures but on the street-front balconies of simpler Spanish Colonial houses. The spacious Bosque house, built for prominent occupants, had (and retains) a wrought-iron monogram on its Chartres Street railing—BB for Bartholome Bosque.

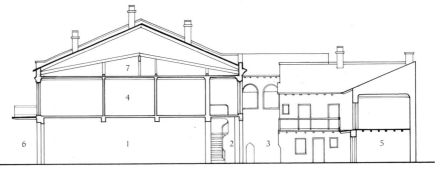

RA6 Bosque house, longitudinal section

RA6 On the ground level, beyond the carriageway wall, was a commercial space, as it is today. The section shows how the carriageway leads past it from Chartres Street to the domestic world of the house. From the loggia one could go through arches into the courtyard or rise to the main rooms on the upper floor. The extensive service structure is L-shaped.

KEY:
1. CARRIAGEWAY
2. LOGGIA
3. COURTYARD
4. RESIDENCE
5. SERVICE ROOMS AND KITCHEN
6. CHARTRES STREET
7. ORIGINAL LOW-PITCHED SPANISH COLONIAL ROOF, LATER COVERED OVER BY A STEEPER ROOF

TYPES

RA7 Chesneau house, 531-33 St. Louis Street, c. 1800 longitudinal section

RA7, RA8, RA9 The Chesneau house is a Spanish Colonial building with all the expected characteristics—a carriageway leading past commercial spaces to a loggia; a loggia that opens through arches to a courtyard; a stairway in the loggia that leads up to residential spaces; a collection of service rooms spaced about the courtyard. For all practical purposes it is a wider, more spacious, version of the Creole townhouse plan, which emerged as something increasingly regularized (and taller) in the nineteenth century. The section shows an entresol that once existed in the house but is now mostly demolished. An entresol is a utilitarian space sandwiched between the ground and second floors of a building. It provided storage for the ground-floor commercial space. Entresols were popular in the late eighteenth and early nineteenth centuries, and a number of other treatments of them developed. See the Creole Town House, p.38.

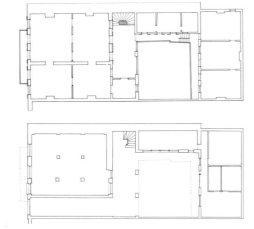

RA8, RA9 Chesneau house, ground and second floor plans

MH67 Chesneau house, 531-33 St. Louis Street, c. 1800

MH67 Alterations have confused the order of the ground floor façade of this house. Probably the original openings would have registered the presence of the entresol.

what most of them have in common, is some version of the sequence of carriageway, loggia, stairway, and courtyard, together with common construction methods and materials and what we might begin to recognize as a shared esthetic. Also, since they tend to be common wall structures, they introduce a new model of urbanity, one which has become an integral part of the Quarter's streetscape.

No Spanish Colonial house is available to us in as pure a state as Madame John's Legacy, but a number survive in altered form. The arrangement of rooms and spaces differs from one example to another. The examples are connected less by a fixed plan than by sets of relationships—of carriageway to loggia, of loggia upward to the residential rooms, of loggia outward to the courtyard, of courtyard to the service rooms. The distinctiveness of the Spanish Colonial house lies in the gelling of these relationships. The relationships, in turn, represent a loose but recognizable synthesis of architectural responses—responses to the pressures of density from a growing population, to the prevailing heat and humidity, and to the cultural predilections of a diverse populace under Spanish rule. These responses need to be examined.

By the close of the Spanish Colonial period, New Orleans had grown in population to about 7,000.[3] After the two great fires of 1788 and 1794 destroyed much of the existing town, brick rather than wood became the construction material of choice and for two-story houses was actually mandated by new ordinances. (In French Colonial times brick had been commonly used, but the availability of wood must have made it the prevalent material for much of the town.) Interior courtyards pressed these new masonry houses to the perimeters of their lots where they shared walls with neighboring buildings. At the street a relatively continuous plane of buildings and walls marked the inner edge of the sidewalk.

At the same time, ways of dealing with the climate became more varied. Carriageways opened up a horizontal shaft in houses through which breezes would be drawn to the courtyard, providing some relief from summer stillness. Builders seem to have drawn their responses to the climate from Spanish and Spanish Colonial building traditions. A preference for arches, usually elliptical, emerged as a way to open walls, especially at loggias. Buildings assumed an appearance of weight and horizontality, emphasized by their limited height; Spanish Colonial houses were never more than two stories, or two stories plus an entresol, because of the real or imagined limits of foundation technology for dealing with New Orleans' high water table.

The roofs on these buildings were tiled, usually of a low pitch. Some were nearly flat and known as terrace roofs. Balustrades of varying material, iron or plastered brick or open tile work, were built at the roof edges. The general effect became weighty and horizontal, relieved by the mullions and muntins of casement windows, doors and elliptically arched fanlights. On these plastered masonry buildings, in clear relief against the planes of their thick walls with their generous, widely-spaced openings, hung light balconies with railings of wrought iron, curled at this period into arabesques, stretched across the street fronts of houses or wrapped around their corners.

MW135 337-343 Royal Street, c. 1800, attributed to Barthélemy Lafon

MW135 *The railing of this Spanish Colonial building has the intricate curves of the most fanciful eighteenth century ironwork.*

RK34 601-07 Chartres Street, c. 1795

RK34 *The terrace roof of this Spanish Colonial house has been altered to become a steeper roof—the gable and its openings were not part of the original house. The walls and cornice curve around the corner, their line repeated by the balcony.*

23

MH72 *In the loggia of a Spanish Colonial house the single Tuscan column stands as a simply rendered recollection of classical forms. Although builders were evidently not concerned with the rigorous demands of building within a classical system, they nevertheless chose to include an occasional column or pilaster.*

MH72 625-27 Chartres Street, c. 1795

The resulting appearance was a marriage; practical responses to problems were wed to a seasoned mixture of cultural preferences. Understood in this way, the esthetic of the Spanish Colonial house is in no way superficial. It was not chosen from a range of possibilities. It is the three-dimensional synthesis of the forces which brought it about. Type and style overlap here in a particular way, a way that gives architectural meaning to the term Creole. If the tall and bony section of the Ursuline Convent reminds us of Norman and Canadian buildings and Madame John's Legacy shows the softening influence of Caribbean galleries, these Spanish Colonial houses have evolved into something lower and heavier, informed by a southern European attitude toward the outside. Colonial ingenuity and urbanism have combined with the organization of a house around some faint echo of water splashing in a classical atrium.

RK35 *Elsewhere in the Bosque house the relief of window muntins or wrought iron railings identify it with other French Quarter buildings. But isolated as they are here, these arched and vaulted shapes speak the common language of simple plastered brick structures in warm climates around the world.*

RK35 Bosque house, 617-19 Chartres Street, 1795

ARH8 detail from wrought iron railing at the Cabildo, c. 1795, Marcellino Hernandez, iron worker

COTTAGE

DATES: BUILT FROM COLONIAL TIMES THROUGH MUCH OF THE NINETEENTH CENTURY

A cottage is a small house. The particular ways cottages were built in the French Quarter responded to the active interplay of local circumstances with the cultural traditions of the builders. They began as simple rectangular boxes with steep hipped roofs, looking like pieces of a French village, spaced apart rather loosely. As the town's density increased and new cultural forces arrived, cottage forms changed.

Eighteenth-century cottages, like earlier buildings in general, had hipped roofs, which are shaped to shed water on all sides. This fact, coupled with a certain visual unity or completeness of form in hipped roof structures, make them especially appropriate for freestanding positions, and in the early town most buildings had plenty of room to stand freely.

A surviving early cottage (usually called Lafitte's Blacksmith Shop after a real or imagined connection with pirate Jean Lafitte) stands on Bourbon Street. The tall roof, especially steep at the ends, retains its original profile except for the cutting back of the overhanging roof and the addition of dormers. The interior layout is also altered, but the position of chimneys shows an original layout of four rooms, each pair sharing a common chimney on the center wall. Simple rectangular openings contain casement doors and windows. Construction is brick between handhewn posts, covered by stucco which is now mostly gone. A wooden kitchen and several outbuildings once sat on the same property. This was a common arrangement in the eighteenth-century French Quarter—several structures and a garden placed loosely about a lot of some 60 by 120 feet. There was variety in the plans of the cottages. Some included a rear

LL11 Lafitte's Blacksmith Shop, 941 Bourbon Street, probably after 1781

LL11, M6 *These two cottages occupied corners three blocks apart. Lafitte's Blacksmith Shop reflects the French Colonial tradition of steep roofs, (the large dormers are later additions.) The other cottage is in the Spanish Colonial tradition, its shallow-pitched roof heavily textured with barrel tiles. Lafitte's has been a bar for many years. The Chartres Street cottage was replaced in this century by a gas station, which gave way to a 1983 residential structure that has since been taken over by a hotel.*

RA10 plan, Lafitte's Shop

M6 1040 Chartres Street, site of building known as the old Spanish cottage. See also MW111, p. 138.

TYPES

M25 *"AN OLD SPANISH HOUSE" is the label on this postcard, c. 1900. The Spanish Colonial date is plausible, judging from its style. The arch occupied by the wagon is probably a carriageway from the street.*

M25 location and date uncertain

gallery set into the body of the house between two small rooms, called *cabinets* (p.116).

As the town's population grew, even these early cottages showed an interesting sense of urbanity. They were built flush with the side-walk and, as in the Lafitte building, had the characteristic *abat-vent*, the overhanging roof which protected both buildings and passersby from rain and intense sun. Tile would have been the usual roofing material, gradually replaced in popularity by slate. A happy architectural consequence of the low, over-hanging, highly textured roofs is the strong presence they have on the street—they seem to come down to meet the pedestrian.

K152 *With its subtly shaped hipped roof, this cottage shows the free-standing nature of early buildings. After decades of commercial use, this building with new additions was converted into a residential complex in 1963.*

K142 *The scale of this L-shaped corner cottage contrasts with the smaller floor heights of its two-story service structure to the left, which opens itself to the street with a balcony.*

K152 1200 Dauphine Street, 1821 or earlier

K142 901 Toulouse Street, probably 1811

M19 *The missing bottom weatherboard reveals the brick-between-post construction of this early cottage. Unable to withstand weather, such construction was covered with stucco or wide, beaded boards, as here. Today this piece of a once-larger cottage survives in an embalmed-looking state attached to a motel.*

RH915 *When built this cottage probably stood free on one side and shared a tall party wall on the other. This accounts for the jaunty asymmetry of its roof.*

M19 609-11 St. Philip Street, c. 1780

RH915 915 St. Philip Street, c. 1825

CREOLE COTTAGE
LATE 1700s UNTIL MID-1800s

A particular cottage type developed in the French Quarter that satisfied the needs of a multitude of domestic situations within the limits of a narrow lot. Such lots were often 32 feet wide, half of the Quarter's original lots of 60 French feet (about 64 modern feet). Creole cottages were limited to such a width, less the narrow passages that were provided on the sides for access to rear yards. Within this dimension a fixed but remarkably versatile plan developed which has remained for two hundred years not only serviceable but a pleasure to live in. The plan, neither small nor large, allows rooms to assume a variety of uses over time.

MW143 address uncertain

LATROBE AND THE CREOLE COTTAGE

In his New Orleans journal architect Benjamin Henry Latrobe remarked on the prevalence of cottages in the old town. He noted cultural variations in how the rooms are used:

March 22d, 1819. New Orleans, beyond Royal street, towards the swamp, retains its old character without variation. The houses are, with hardly a dozen exceptions among many hundred, one-story houses… These one-storied houses are very simple in their plan. The two front rooms open into the street with French glass doors. Those on one side are the dining & drawing rooms, the others, chambers. The front rooms, when inhabited by Americans, are the family rooms, & the back rooms the chambers.

Benjamin Henry Latrobe
Impressions Respecting New Orleans
Diary & Sketches, 1818-1820[4]

Latrobe implies that placing the bedrooms to one side is Creole (as opposed to American) practice. That arrangement allows for passage through the house without disturbing the bedrooms and without a hall. The lack of halls is characteristic of New Orleans houses prior to the arrival of Americans. With a clever arrangement of rooms, privacy was possible without them. The Creole cottage plan was also readily adaptable for double occupancy by dividing the house down the center, the same strategy as the plan of the later shotgun double. Each side would have access to both the street and the courtyard but not, in this case, with perfect privacy.

RK87 822-24 St. Ann Street

TYPES

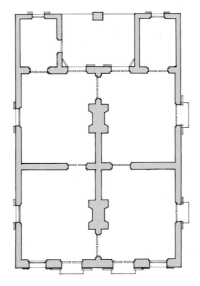

RA11 plan of La Rionda-Correjolles house, 1218-1220 Burgundy Street, constructed between 1810 and 1812

RK17, K136B, K136A *The La Rionda-Correjolles cottage has the low, dormerless profile of early Creole cottages. Note the subtle double pitch of the roof. The raised cabinets have aboveground cellars beneath them. They flank an arched gallery. The two-story service structure sits parallel to the main cottage separated from it by a courtyard.*

RK17 La Rionda-Correjolles house

K136B service structure

K136A view of rear and side

As a type the Creole cottage is very clear. It is a house of one-and-a-half stories with a gabled roof, the ridge of which is parallel to the street. The floor is raised some 18 to 30 inches above a ventilated crawl space. There are four squarish interconnecting rooms sharing two chimneys. Except for the smallest examples there is, behind the four rooms, an additional range of three spaces facing a rear yard. The largest of these is a gallery or porch in the center which is open to the yard or, sometimes, glassed in. At either end are two enclosed service spaces, roughly square, known as *cabinets* (pp. 114-15). The cabinets open to the gallery and sometimes to the other rooms. The cabinet floors may be raised several feet, with the space below used as a kind of above-ground cellar, accessible from the rear. In cottages where the attic is finished, a stair is provided in one of the cabinets.

Across the street front of the Creole cottage are four shuttered openings, at least two of which are casement doors. The other two may also be casement doors or may be casement or double-hung windows. Casements are the earlier solution; double-hung windows begin to appear on cottages around 1820. The arrangement of openings is symmetrical—either door-window-window-door or window-door-door-window.

Assuming that the rear gallery is open or at least openable, each room in this layout connects to the outside on two sides. With both windows and shutters on each opening, the possibilities for varying light, ventilation and privacy from room to room are extensive. Rooms can be used for a variety of purposes, and they can change purposes from time to time. The gallery can be either a room or a porch or a workspace. The casement doors on the front maintain the possibility of discourse

CABLE AND THE CREOLE COTTAGE

George Washington Cable (1844-1925) often set his tales within specific New Orleans buildings which he observed with a fine eye. His Madame Delphine, in a story of the same name, inhabited what is unmistakably a Creole cottage:

... as you begin to find the way a trifle more open, you will not fail to notice on the righthand side, about midway of the square, a small, low, brick house of a story and a half, set out upon the sidewalk, as weatherbeaten and mute as an aged beggar fallen asleep. Its corrugated roof of dull red tiles, sloping down toward you with an inward curve, is overgrown with weeds, and in the fall of the year is gay with the yellow plumes of the goldenrod. You can almost touch with your cane the low edge of the broad, overhanging eaves. The batten shutters at door and window, with hinges like those of a postern, are shut with a grip that makes one's knuckles and nails feel lacerated. Save in the brickwork itself there is not a cranny. You would say the house has the lockjaw. There are two doors, and to each a single chipped and battered marble step. Continuing on down the sidewalk, on a line with the house, is a garden masked from view by a high, close board fence. You may see the tops of its fruit trees—pomegranate, peach, banana, fig, pear, and particularly one large orange, close by the fence, that must be very old.
  "Madame Delphine,"
  Old Creole Days[5]

The term "Creole cottage" is a classification made after the fact. "Creole" refers to the mixed culture, principally French, African and Spanish, of the colonial period. It distinguishes that culture from the American culture which came only gradually to rival and dominate it during the course of the nineteenth century. But coined after the fact or not, "Creole cottage" goes back at least as far as Cable's story, "Café des Exilés" from *Old Creole Days*, published in 1879. Cable set his story decades earlier, in 1835. It is an interesting coincidence that the exiles of the title who gather at this café come from Santo Domingo, Barbados, Martinique, and Cuba, possible architectural sources for the Creole cottage. The scene of the story is

An antiquated story-and-a-half Creole cottage sitting right down on the banquette, as do the Choctaw squaws who sell bay and sassafras and life everlasting, with a high, close board fence shutting out of view the diminutive garden on the southern side.
  "Café des Exilés"
  Old Creole Days[6]

Lafcadio Hearn (1850-1904) identified specific buildings Cable described in an 1883 essay "The Scenes of Cable's Romances." He placed the Café des Exilés on "the west side of Rampart Street" and reported its recent demolition "to make room, no doubt, for some modern architectural platitude."[7] Early preservationist sentiments. Would Hearn wince to know that such "platitudes" of the 1880s are now preserved nearly as carefully as the kind of cottages they replaced?

RH917 Gaillard cottage, 915-17 St. Ann Street, 1824, detail

TYPES

MW145 823-25 Bourbon Street, c. 1830

MW145 *Plaster banding, a pan-tile roof and elaborate transoms distinguish this cottage.*

K217 *Creole cottages were often adapted for commercial use.*

RK105B *This early cottage with elegant transoms and a metal abat-vent sits next to a later, taller Creole cottage.*

RK101 *(detail) Double-hung windows began to replace casements about 1820.*

K217 address uncertain

RK101 823-25 St. Philip, c. 1821

RK105B 931-33 St. Philip Street, 1805

with the street—these can be very public dwellings and have often been used commercially—or quite private when the shutters are closed. The rear gallery draws the private attentions of the residents to the rear yard, which takes on some qualities of a room itself. The rear yard of a Creole cottage is called a courtyard as if it were surrounded by buildings and walls in the manner of a Spanish Colonial house. Indeed, it often is.

The Creole cottage type seems to have begun in the Spanish Colonial period. It continued through much of the nineteenth century; the Vieux Carré Survey points out one modified example built as late as 1880. The early ones are identifiable by relatively lower room heights, the use of casement rather than double-hung windows, and the absence of dormers. Early Creole cottages, as well as the smaller ones built later, may be only four rooms. They are similar to still earlier cottages of the colonial period, but are distinguished by their gabled rather than hipped roofs. Both Samuel Wilson, Jr., and Jay D. Edwards refer to similarities between the New Orleans Creole cottage and houses built on the island of Hispaniola (modern Haiti and the Dominican Republic).[8,9] It is striking that large numbers of these cottages were built in the early nineteenth century, the same time that several thousand refugees from the slave uprisings on Hispaniola were being assimilated into New Orleans. The full influence of these arrivals on local architecture remains to be appreciated.

Creole cottages have been the dominant French Quarter house in sheer numbers. Modest to start with, they evolved to attain a refinement of scale and detail equal to larger town houses. Their casement doors may be surmounted with transoms showing elegantly curved muntins, their galleries may be enclosed with delicate fanlights, their mantels may be beautifully carved, their dormers may be subtly proportioned and crafted.

Creole cottages became taller and larger as the nineteenth century progressed. Ceiling heights increased, and, to the extent the lots permitted, rooms grew in size. The attic space came to be finished, illuminated by dormers, and used. Such houses, commonly built with a separate two-story kitchen and service building, became commodious.

The narrow lots were relatively deep, normally 120 feet or so. The cottage might be 40 to 50 feet deep, leaving 70 to 80 feet for a rear yard and one or more outbuildings. The most common arrangement provided a separate two-story structure one room deep across the rear of the property. Such a service structure might contain a kitchen, other service spaces and bedrooms for family members, slaves or servants. The yard between the two principal buildings could take on much the same shape and character as the courtyard of the Spanish Colonial house or later town houses. Its principal uses were undoubtedly utilitarian. Sometimes a service structure might be moved closer to the house, perhaps with an arch through its ground floor, allowing for a second courtyard. Other times service structures were built as attached ells or as multiple structures in different arrangements. Access to service structures was generally across the courtyard, and the relationship between inside and outside spaces was intimate and refined.

Sometimes Creole cottages were built in groups, revealing an urban sensibility not evident in earlier cottages. When several identical cottages sit on the street in a row, with the narrowest of passages between them, they look like pastries on a cookie sheet, cut

RA12 Section, La Rionda cottage, 1218-20 Burgundy Street, 1810-1812

RA13 section, Creole cottage with habitable upper level

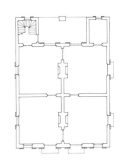

RA14 larger Creole cottage plan.

RA12, RA13, and K29
Gradually the ceiling heights of Creole cottages increased and their roof pitches became steeper, allowing generous finished rooms in the upper floor. Dormers opened the upper rooms to light and ventilation. Stairs in one of the cabinets provided access.

K29 625 Dauphine Street

31

TYPES

MH84 *The roof of the end cottage in this row of three is hipped to acknowledge its postion on a street corner. Its* abat-vent *follows the roof around the corner, shading the walls and sheltering passersby.*

MH84 1031-1043 Chartres Street, c. 1824

apart and separated just far enough to retain their identity. When such a row reaches a corner the roof of the end house is hipped on one side to acknowledge its frontage on two streets. It is hard to imagine any reason for this pattern but an urban consciousness—practically, the hipped roof only diminishes attic space.

The visual effect of a row of parallel gabled roofs rounding the corner on a hipped angle is an effective piece of street design, appearing almost poignant to the modern eye.

RK89B *Two arches rest on a simple column, opening the gallery at the rear of the Gaillard cottage. A pair of separate, small, two-story service structures is symmetrically arranged, their balconies overlooking the courtyard. Residents move freely between many different degrees of enclosure.*

RK89B Gaillard cottage, rear view, 915-17 St. Ann Street, 1824

NARROWER COTTAGES

The usual Creole cottage was sometimes a "double," with the two halves separately occupied. It followed, then, that half of such a house could be built freestanding. This produced a two-bay house, with striking contrast between the narrow front, with its dormer, and the tall gabled side. When a third bay was added, the proportions became less extreme, curiously graceful, in fact. The door in the third bay opened into a corridor or sometimes a side gallery. This is perhaps an exception to the Creole avoidance of halls, and perhaps a case of American influence. When open as a side gallery, however, the third bay became not so much a hall as an additional "in-between space," the kind of refined negotiation between inside and outside that is typical of Creole buildings. Such a plan also invites comparison with the the Charleston side-galleried house. The similarity of the two plans is probably less a matter of cultural borrowing than of similar solutions to a similar problem, separately devised.

M9 location uncertain

M9 Looking as if it might be the remaining half of a sliced Creole cottage, this house has the normal accoutrement—abat-vent, batten shutters, casement doors, generous vertical dimensions and a dormer to illuminate the upper floor.

K134 Seeing daylight through the glass panel in the front door of this three-bay cottage reveals that the door opens not to the interior of the house but to a side gallery.

M23 This view, resembling a longitudinal section cut through this house, shows the substantial volume enclosed within such a narrow cottage. The two-story building behind appears to be this building's service structure.

K134 1122 Burgundy Street, 1826

M23 address uncertain

33

TYPES

CL27 1012-14 Dauphine Street, 1826

CL27 *The center arch, lower than the others, marks an open passage through the house. At its top is an open barred transom.*

K118 *The center door of this cottage leads to the interior. The doorway between two pairs of double-hung windows has an American look to it. But the cottage retains the traditional end gables and metal abat-vent of the Creole cottage.*

K135 *The arrangement of six openings marks this as a triple cottage. The hipped roof at the near end acknowledges the turn of the corner.*

K101 *Showing its gabled end to Bourbon Street, this triple cottage has each segment marked by a dormer. The post-supported roof wrapping the corner and the corner doorway were added to reorient the building to Bourbon Street.*

WIDER COTTAGES

Cottages of five bays were sometimes built, and a few remain. The center bay usually provided circulation, either to the rear yard via an open-ended passage or, as a front door, to an interior hall. In the latter instance, one expects to find a center hall through the house with symmetrical rooms arranged on either side. Such a plan is common elsewhere in New Orleans and throughout the South, but is not usually the case in the Quarter. Here is another example of resistance to the use of enclosed halls by Creole builders (though there are fine examples of Creole *town houses* with center halls on the second floor).

A triple cottage or even a quadruple cottage could be built on especially wide lots. An open passageway might be inserted beside middle units in order to give separate access to their rear yards.

K118 915 Bourbon Street, c. 1845-50, possibly the remodeling of an 1827 cottage

K135 1137-41 Burgundy Street, c. 1825

K101 341 Bourbon Street

34

TALLER COTTAGES

In the later development of the Creole cottage dormers and higher roofs increased the habitable volume. But earlier cottages had achieved a similar result by extending the walls upward. Several examples remain of the "one-and-three-quarters cottage", a version in which the ground floor walls rise three or four feet above the attic floor, effectively raising the roof and expanding the very low spaces at the edges of the attic which were otherwise unusable. Instead of dormers, low, wide casements were placed in the extended walls, not unlike the windows which later became popular for the attics of Greek Revival town houses.

When still more space was desired, two-story cottages were built. Few of these are found in the Quarter, perhaps because they, with their service structures, quickly approached the volume of a town house. In form they are similar to the town house, but the arrangement of four bays across the front and the end-gabled roof place them within the cottage type. The clearer examples are also free-standing.

RH819 817-19 St. Ann Street, c. 1811

RH819, RK86A *Building taller walls was one way to increase the volume of the Creole cottage. Small horizontally-shaped windows provide air and light to the upper floor. The cabinets on the rear side are split into two levels so that at those points the little house has three distinct floors.*

MH36 *In this two-story Creole cottage, two conventional façades are stacked, with a balcony at the second level. Like the usual one-story cottage, this house is gabled at the side. It does not share a party wall on either side, though it is built to the property line on the lake side.*

MH36 814 Gov. Nicholls Street, c. 1830

RK86A 817-19 St. Ann Street, rear, c. 1811

TYPES

RK66 928-32 Gov. Nicholls Street, c. 1831

DEEPER COTTAGES

Long rectangular cottages with their shorter face on the street are rare but occur on several sites in the Quarter. They are one room wide, several rooms deep and have hipped roofs. Their shape and arrangement of rooms invite comparison to the shotgun house type. Several of these houses have been cited in support of a theory put forward by John Michael Vlach that the New Orleans shotgun house evolved from an African house form. According to the theory, the African type was built on the island of Hispaniola, then brought to New Orleans by refugees from the slave uprisings there. These long French Quarter cottages are seen as evidence that the basic form was actually built here, at least occasionally, in the period just after the influx of the refugees in the late eighteenth and early nineteenth centuries. The theory is discussed further on page 48.

RK66 *These two houses are hipped in such a way as to lean aganist adjacent party walls. Positioned at the edges of their lots, each can open its long side to the space between them which becomes relatively generous and open to light.*

RK67 *The plan of this free-standing cottage consists of five rooms lined up perpendicular to the street. Simple plaster bands mark the sides and top of the façade. There is a molded plaster cornice just below the metal abat-vent.*

K8 *Solid paneled shutters lie open beside the doors of this hip-roofed cottage. It has a metal abat-vent and the plaster banding typical of buildings of the late eighteenth and early nineteenth centuries.*

RK67 1024 Gov. Nicholls Street, 1826 or earlier

K8 819 Burgundy Street, c. 1810

TOWN HOUSE
DATES: BUILT THROUGHOUT THE 1800s

The French Quarter town house is identified most tellingly by a set of urban attitudes. Under the pressure of increasing population, plus a degree of cultural pressure from the influx of Anglo-Americans, the loosely organized Spanish Colonial house was regularized into a more compact house type. The type was repeated again and again throughout the district, as well as beyond it in the expanding city. We use the term town house to identify this type as it was built in the nineteenth century, the period when it became regularized and identifiable.

The town house has two faces—a regular public one confronting and overlooking the street with predictable openings and balconies, and a softer, more individualized private one surrounding and protecting its courtyard. The town house is generally a row house in the sense that it extends out to one or both of its side property lines where it may share a wall with a neighboring building. Sometimes it is also a row house in the sense of being part of a continuous row of similar houses constructed by a single builder.

Regularization of the type happened as the population and prosperity of the town surged in the decades following 1803, the year when Thomas Jefferson, through the Louisiana Purchase agreement, acquired New Orleans and the entire Louisiana Territory for the United States. The gradual architectural regularization can be seen as a trend toward standardization, itself a result of the increased pace of construction in New Orleans. More and more of the town's original lots were subdivided lengthwise, retaining their depth but losing width. The result was a consolidation of the type to fit narrower lots. With consolidation came a refinement of its parts and perhaps an increasing consciousness of style.

MW137 The uptown corner of Royal and Dumaine Streets

The French Quarter town house is at least two stories tall. It seldom goes above three-and-a-half. Its façade is from three to five bays wide. Balconies and galleries extend principal upstairs rooms out over sidewalks. Within is a courtyard, often narrow, bounded by a configuration of smaller rooms connected by balconies; balconies are used for communication between rooms. Roofs of the main house are usually hipped or gabled (with the ridge parallel to the street). There may be dormers or not. Service structures of two to three stories may be connected to the main house or separate. They have shed roofs sloping inward to the courtyard where their water was collected in cisterns.

Under the category of town house we include the Creole town house type as well as an American variant more like town houses on the Eastern Seaboard. The two will be explored separately.

MW137 *The two buildings opposite each other at this intersection reveal the development of the town house over a thirty-year period. At left is 838-42 Royal, a two-story house of c. 1805. Its double-pitched roof extends over the balcony which wraps the building on three sides. Across the street is 841 Royal, a three-story house of c. 1833. It is larger and more conscious of refinement in its detail. Its taller stature is not only a matter of the additional story but also of the greater ceiling heights inside. Both these buildings have stores on their ground floors and residences above. Both fit within the category of Creole, as opposed to American, town houses.*

TYPES

RT1 *Uncertainty about soil conditions had limited most colonial structures to two stories so, even without the added top floor, this house was tall for its time. It was built at the beginning of a transition from two- to three-story houses, probably emboldening other builders. George Washington Cable set his story "Sieur George" here, and "Sieur George's house" is one of several names by which it is known.*

RT1 Pedesclaux-Le Monnier house, 636-40 Royal Street, designed c. 1794, completed 1811, fourth floor later; probably designed by Barthelemy Lafon and completed by Latour and Laclotte

RA15 Pedesclaux Le Monnier house, plan of ground level

RA15, RA16 *The courtyard, the loggia with its stair and the upper levels are entered through a passage from Royal Street. The elliptical salon and the other two principal rooms open to individual balconies.*

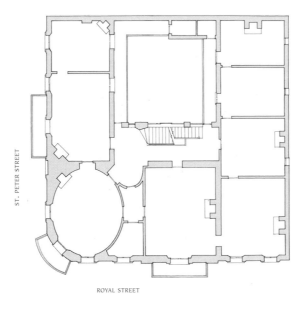

ST. PETER STREET

ROYAL STREET

RA16 Pedesclaux-Le Monnier house, plan of third level

CREOLE TOWN HOUSE

Tradition, myth and its abundance have made the Creole town house the quintessential French Quarter building. The components of carriage-way, loggia, courtyard and balcony are integrated most completely in it. The type developed from the Spanish Colonial house. Its development can be traced by considering two specific town houses completed during the decades just after the Louisiana Purchase. These two "transitional" houses and others like them are some of the Quarter's most interesting structures, built on large lots like Spanish Colonial residences, but increasing their volume by growing taller.

The Pedesclaux-Le Monnier house, begun around 1794 but not completed until 1811, overlaps the Colonial and American periods. On the Royal Street façade the cornice projects over a central bay with a balcony, somewhat in the manner of the Chesneau house (p. 22) or 417 Royal Street, now Brennan's restaurant. Here the projection is marked with pilasters. The low second floor could fit into the category of an entresol, another similarity to the Chesneau house. But it is enough like a separate floor to identify this house's chief difference from Spanish Colonial buildings—its greater height. Even though the fourth floor is a later addition, the verticality of the first three floors set the building apart in its day. That a building as important as the Cabildo had been limited to two floors demonstrates builders' traditional fear of swampy soil conditions. Increased verticality typifies later town houses— the force of an expanding population pressed the house in at its sides, forcing it upwards.

In plan this house exploits its corner site by opening principal rooms onto each street. (The courtyard is entered from Royal Street.) The elliptical salon is an unexpected flourish—an idea from Paris, perhaps, or from England via the East Coast.

The Napoleon House of 1814 also straddles the two centuries. It consists of a three-story addition to a smaller six-bay Spanish Colonial structure built two decades earlier. The jump to three full stories plus a high roof and cupola must have been dramatic in 1814, emboldening other town house builders to follow suit. The architect of the three-story part was probably French-born Hyacinthe Laclotte, who also worked at the Pedesclaux-Le Monnier house. He again took advantage of a generous corner site, integrating his addition with the existing two-story house of 1798. The addition has considerably more volume than the pre-existing house, but it occupies less site. It places a new loggia and stairway adjacent to the earlier structure's courtyard. The principal rooms face the streets on both sides, and service rooms open within. The original building's carriageway from St. Louis Street is retained; the new portion has only a narrow passage from Chartres Street. The rooms on the second floor have handsome wooden mantels and other millwork, refinements showing the requirements of New Orleanians at this time (as well as at various times before and since)—tall, nicely shaped rooms which respond to the climate with large, shuttered doors and windows, all with at least a soupçon of Gallic style.

A somewhat intensified urbanity has forced the buildings upwards. The weighty, horizontal Spanish Colonial massing has been replaced with lighter-footed shapes. And New Orleans' affinity for French fashion has reappeared. (Napoleon's popularity in New Orleans accounts for the house's sobriquet which still survives). There is still, however, a reluctance to tighten the plan; the Napoleon house spreads out on its site with an easy grace remembered from the Spanish Colonial period.

RA17 Napoleon House, longitudinal section

RA18 Napoleon House, ground floor plan

CHARTRES STREET

ST. LOUIS STREET

RA19 second floor plan

RA17, RA18, RA19 *The newer three-story block of this house has a steep roof with an octagonal cupola. Its tall and upright stance sets it apart from its Spanish Colonial predecessors (and the Spanish Colonial house to which it was added). There is a carriageway entrance to the courtyard from St. Louis Street and a narrower passage to the loggia from Chartres Street.*

Room key :
1. CARRIAGEWAY
2. PASSAGE
3. COURTYARD
4. LOGGIA
5. RESIDENCE
6. SERVICE ROOMS AND KITCHEN
7. COMMERCIAL

RH500A *The Napoleon House is also known as the Girod house after its builder, Mayor Nicholas Girod.*

RH500A Napoleon House, 500-06 Chartres Street, two-story wing facing St. Louis street built 1798; three-story block built 1814; Hyacinthe Laclotte, probable architect.

TYPES

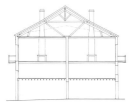

RA20 Section and elevation, 514-518 Toulouse Street, c. 1818

RA20 The section shows the position of the entresol, sandwiched between the commercial ground floor and the residence above. Today part of the entresol survives, part has been removed. Dotted lines show the original low-pitched roof. On the elevation, five residential openings are spaced above three arches. The left one is a carriageway.

M26 This three-story Creole town house includes an entresol, the floor of which aligns with the spring points of the arches. Architect DePouilly arrived from France in 1833 and began construction on the St. Louis Hotel (across the street from this house) in 1835. The arches of this plastered brick house recall the granite arches of the hotel.

HC3 The clear cubic geometry of this building is evident in this corner photograph. Arches about twelve feet tall provide light for the ground floor and entresol levels.

M26 Dufilho Pharmacy, now the Pharmacy Museum, 514-516 Chartres Street, 1837, J. N. B. DePouilly, probable architect

HC3 Old Absinthe House Bar, 234-240 Bourbon Street, c. 1806

The entresol is sometimes a component of the town house and deserves consideration. It is a low-ceilinged storage or service floor placed above the commercial first level and connected with it. The Chesneau house of c. 1800 was built with such a level, and a number of houses with entresols survive from the early decades of the nineteenth century. A favorite treatment of the entresol between 1800 and 1820 combines both ground floor and entresol behind one set of tall arched openings which face the street; the entresol floor coincides with the arches' springpoints. The entresol's windows are the semi-circular tops of the arches, fitted with operable sashes hinged as casements. The actual second floor, the residential level, has casement doors of a noticeably smaller scale opening to a balcony. After 1820 or so, an entresol was generally expressed on the façade as a separate, low story with its own rectangular casement openings.

The 1820s and 30s were a prosperous and lively time in New Orleans. Antagonism between Creoles and Americans was so strong that in 1836 three separate municipalities were established within the city. The French Quarter was the First Municipality, and remained dominated by Creoles. French influence had not only its traditional hegemony in Creole culture. Archivist and historian Sally Reeves has noted that Gallic partisanship was actually strengthened after Colonial times by thousands of refugees from Hispaniola who spoke French and had French customs.[10] It was further reinforced by nineteenth-century immigrants from France, including several architects. Yet American influence in New Orleans was also strong and strengthening. It was dominant, in fact, on the upriver side of Canal Street. It is these strongly conflicting forces which were eventually forced into a particularly New Orleanian synthesis—a regularized three-bay

row house, its façade within the traditions of East Coast cities, but its street level used commercially, its residential zone entered through an open side passage rather than the American hall, and a rear stairway located in a loggia adjacent to a courtyard. The conflicted process by which Creoles assimilated American influence became architecturally manifest in the large number of Creole townhouses built in the French Quarter during the 1830s.

In other words, the regularity that emerged in the Creole town house—houses had not been so much alike in colonial times—is American influence, even at the same moment that the Creole town house holds its own against the more closed American type. The Creole town house has the openness and lack of façade pretension of earlier French Quarter houses, combined with a recognizable identity of type. But it successfully resists the more enclosed, weather-proof personality of the American East Coast house. It does not loose the wonderfully subtle gradations between inside and outside established by its traditional devices of dealing with the climate.

What are the characteristics of this regularized type? Stylistically, full-length arched openings are preferred for the street level. Though three bays are normal, there are fine five-bay examples as well as other variants. A carriage-way, gated at the street and open at the rear, passes the commercial ground floor rooms and leads to an open loggia from which a stair rises to the residential quarters. In smaller versions the carriageway may be reduced to a narrow flagstone passage open at the courtyard end but secured with a door with perhaps an unglazed barred transom at the street. Runnels carved into the flagstones may channel water from the courtyard to the street. The loggia, open to the courtyard at the ground level, often

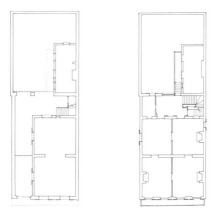

RA21 Nicolas house, 723 Toulouse Street, 1808, Hilaire Boutté, builder

K147 901-05-07 Dauphine, c. 1833

RA21 This plan and section are an early instance of the regularized two-story Creole town house. Later, in the 1820s and 30s, many houses similar in plan were built, often three-stories tall. Note the similarity between this second floor plan and that of the Creole cottage (pp. 14, 17).

K147 The corner Creole town house of this row of three has two rather than three openings. Its corner position obviates the passage the others need to reach their courtyards because there is a door from the side street giving direct access to the loggia.

TYPES

RH536ChA *Looking at the side of the Gally houses, one can imagine the sequence of rooms shown in the plans below. On each upper level are two rooms, plus a glassed-in loggia at the rear. The loggia overlooks the narrow courtyard through arched windows. The open loggia at ground level would increase the apparent size of the courtyard. The tall service structure stretches across the rear of the three houses. Access to the private areas of the inner two houses is through the arched doorway in the base of the service structure. The kitchens, in this case, must have been on the second level of the service structure. The ground-floor spaces in the front were used commercially.*

RA22 *These three unusually narrow Creole town houses have no carriageways. Instead, a common passage extends to each unit from the side street through the rear of the service structure.*

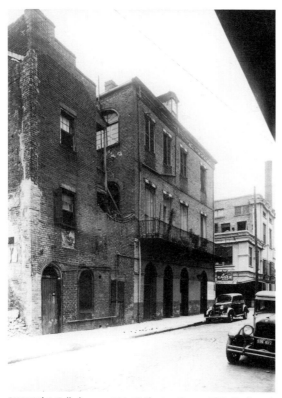

RH536ChA Gally houses, 536-40 Chartres Street, 1830, Gurlie and Guillot. This side view is from Toulouse Street.

has sash in the upper level openings which are commonly arched, allowing for fanlights, a favorite device. Attics, formed by trussed roofs of fairly steep slope, may be illuminated by dormers with arched sash, divided into gracefully-shaped panes by curving wood muntins.

There is generally a depth of no more than two residential rooms in the front block—one opening to the street, one to the loggia. Openings are typically casement doors or paired panel doors with decorative transoms. Two or three stories of smaller rooms (originally kitchens, slaves' or servants' quarters, rooms for boys of the household, storerooms, privies, occasionally stables) skirt one edge of the courtyard or form an ell around it. Such a service wing is often connected to the loggia by balconies, but is sometimes entirely separate. When ceilings are taller in the front structure and lower behind, floor levels do not necessarily align. A short run of steps may energize a balcony connecting the levels.

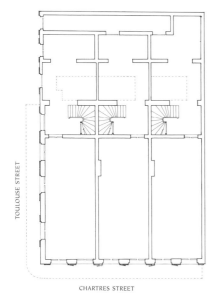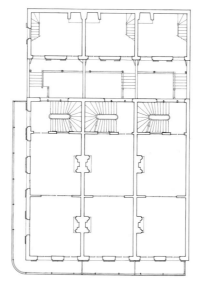

TOULOUSE STREET

CHARTRES STREET

RA22 Gally houses, ground floor plans (left) and second floor plans, original configuration

CL33 2700 block of Royal Street

CL33 *This rear view of an isolated Creole town house makes clear its formal arrangement—front block, service wing, and walled courtyard. Clarence Laughlin photographed this example, now demolished, outside the Quarter in the Faubourg Marigny.*

The Pontalba buildings on Jackson Square occupy an interesting juncture between Creole and American town house design. When they were completed in 1850, facing each other across the city's principal square, they elevated the row house to a prominence unprecedented in New Orleans. Built at a time when Creole influence had waned dramatically, built with red brick and granite (imported American materials), and innovative in their introduction to New Orleans of the large-scale use of cast iron, the Pontalba houses were still fundamentally Creole. Commercial uses lined the street level. Residences above were entered through flagstone passageways leading to a stair hall behind the commercial spaces. The plans of these town houses reflected the traditional proclivities of the woman who built them, a rich Creole with strong Parisian ties.

CL2, RT15 *The Pontalba town houses were organized around individual courtyards. Typically Creole, each house contained a ground floor commercial use with two residential floors and an attic above. Today most of these houses are subdivided into apartments.*

CL 2 Lower Pontalba Building from the cupola of the Cabildo

RT15 Lower Pontalba Buildings, St. Ann Street at Jackson Square, 1849-50, James Gallier, Sr., original architect, Henry Howard, architect of final plans. This view is from the Presbytère.

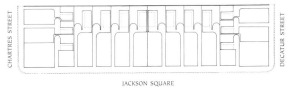

RA23 *The Pontalba Buildings line the two block faces to the upriver and downriver sides of Jackson Square. End units turn the corners onto Chartres and Decatur Streets.*

Room Key
1. COMMERCIAL SPACE
2. ENTRY TO RESIDENCE
3. COURTYARD
4. KITCHEN
5. SERVICE ROOM/SMALL BEDROOM
6. PARLOR
7. DINING ROOM
8. BEDROOM
9. PRIVY

RA23 Site plan, floor plans of the original layout of the Pontalba town houses

TYPES

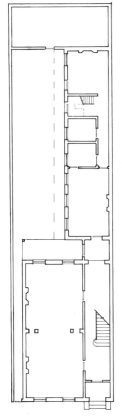

RA24 Plan of a typical American town house

K177 pair of American town houses, address uncertain

AMERICAN TOWN HOUSE

The American preference was for a closed hall in place of an open carriageway. Like the row houses of East Coast cities, the American town house was entirely residential, without the ground floor commercial space typical of the Creole houses. The stairway often ran along one side of the hall instead of rising at the end of a loggia. As early as 1819 Benjamin Henry Latrobe noted, with distinct reservations, the increasing popularity of this type in New Orleans (p. 45). The American plan became especially popular during the booming pre-Civil War decades of the 1840s and 50s. Some of the grandest examples of these houses are on Bourbon Street, many now disfigured by a succession of night club usages. Others are modest.

The typical American town house was three bays wide and sat on an average French Quarter lot, about thirty-two feet in width. However a certain amount of experimentation occurred in their design—some had wide lots and stables, and some became large free-standing establishments.

K130 *A brick front and a raised doorway to a side hall identify this as a clear example of the American town house. Sliding sashes on all the front windows further identify the type.*

MH4 *Some of the largest American town houses were built on upper Bourbon Street. This one has a horizontally rusticated granite base and granite trim on the upper openings.*

K92 *This corner view suggests the substantial volume of the three-story-plus-attic town house. The top level could have full-height rooms under the roof ridge with ancillary spaces under the eaves.*

K189B *Red brick was the preferred material for the American town house. Here a more expensive brick laid in a Flemish bond on the front of this house changes to a common brick on the sides.*

K89 *When the Second Empire style was in fashion (c. 1880 in the French Quarter) a town house could have a mansard roof such as this. It allowed a large third floor which looked more like an attic from outside.*

K130 817 Burgundy, c. 1840

MH4 Rouzan house, 522 Bourbon Street, c. 1840, possibly by James Gallier, Sr.

K92 address uncertain

K189B 1014-16 St. Louis Street, 1831, Daniel Twogood, builder

K89 1027-31 Bienville Street, date uncertain, demolished

LATROBE ON SIDE HALLS AND RED BRICK
Benjamin Henry Latrobe perceived with some regret the rise of American building practices in New Orleans. He wrote in his diary in 1819:

But this much I must say, that altho' the sort of house built here by the French is not the best specimen of French arrangement, yet it is infinitely, in my opinion, superior to that arrangement which we have inherited from the English. But so inveterate is habit that the merchants from the old United States, who are daily gaining ground on the manners, the habits, the opinions, & the domestic arrangments of the French, have already begun to introduce the detestable, lop-sided, London house, in which a common passage & stairs acts as a common sewer to all the necessities of the dwelling & renders it impossible to preserve a temperature within the house materially different from that of the atmosphere, as the coughs, colds, & consumptions of our Eastern cities amply tesitfy. With the English arrangement, the red brick fronts are also gaining ground, & the suburb St. Mary, the American suburb, already exhibits the flat, dull, dingy character of Market Street, in Philadelphia, or [a] Baltimore street, instead of the motley & picturesque effect of the stuccoed French buildings of the city. We shall introduce many grand & profitable improvements, but they will take the place of much elegance, ease, & some convenience.

Benjamin Henry Latrobe
Impressions Respecting New Orleans
Diary & Sketches 1818-1820[11]

K194B Taney house, 908 St. Louis Street, 1834, Edward William Sewell, builder

K194B *The Taney house is a proper American town house. A carefully detailed doorway leads into a hallway. The house shares a common wall with its neighbor to the right. Because the lot is wider than usual, there is space to the left for a small side yard functional, in this case, as a driveway into a larger-than-average lot. This house has two stories plus an attic, but taller examples of the American town house type extend upward to three stories.*

MH62 *The American town house type persisted during the second half of the nineteenth century. This urbane Italianate example has the usual lower-ceiling service ell attached at the rear.*

K13 *François Correjolles, architect of the Beauregard House (p.46), is believed to have built this town house for himself. He used an American plan with side hall but covered the brick with stucco in the Creole way.*

LL19 *Twenty-five years after the Beauregard House, de Pouilly constructed this variation on its front façade. Another variant is at 524 Esplanade Avenue, an 1845 version designed in the Greek Revival style.*

MH62 547 Esplanade Avenue, 1879, William Fitzner, architect; P. R. Middlemiss, builder

K13 1216 Burgundy Street c. 1831, François Correjolles, architect;

LL19 521 Dauphine, 1851, J.N.B. de Pouilly

45

TYPES

MW109 Beauregard House, 1101-13 Chartres Street, 1826, François Correjolles, architect, James Lambert, builder

MW109 Looking at the façade of the Beauregard House, one wonders if Correjolles might have known Palladio's far grander Villa Foscari, with its twin stairs and temple front. This house could sit comfortably with acres of land around it. It seems a rural type, but two other houses in the Quarter attempt a similar strategy (photograph, p. 45).

RA25 Correjolles' plan combines American and Creole characteristics—a wide center hall leads to a cabinet/gallery arrangement at the rear. The plan shows the current condition: the original gallery has been enclosed and another added beyond it.

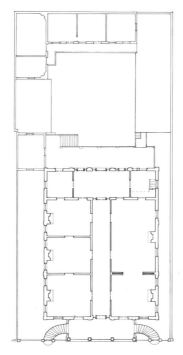

RA25 Beauregard House, plan

Among non-conformists within the American town house type, there are three that represent distinct and interesting departures from the norm. All have become house museums.

The Beauregard House is a special puzzle. The entrance is set within a broad raised gallery with stairs leading up from the street at either end. Double doors open to a wide center hall, a space one associates with the American tradition and, because of its generous dimensions, with the South. The hall terminates in a space perpendicular to it with smaller rooms at either end. That central space, now the dining room, was originally an open gallery with cabinets in the Creole tradition. Drawings survive showing an earlier plan for this house with no center hall and a narrower elevation. Interestingly awkward, these drawings seem to be grappling with the problem of how to graft a center hall, a fifth bay and a front gallery onto what might otherwise be an enlarged Creole cottage plan. One seems to be witnessing a struggle between building types.

The Hermann-Grima House is similarly a marriage of types. It sits apart from its neighbors, foursquare and American. Its brick is unplastered (though now painted and "lined"). Each floor has a center hall with a stairway. However, there is a balcony on the front. And at the rear, as in the Beauregard House, is a gallery with cabinets, here repeated on the second level. In the spacious courtyard is a three-story service structure, freestanding like an escapee from a more conventional French Quarter house.

Architect James Gallier, Jr., made his own house at 1132 Royal Street a hybrid between the Creole town house (there is a carriageway leading to a courtyard) and the American town house, characterized by an enclosed side hall. A straight stair climbs one wall of the hall, but there is a loggia-like back porch at the end of the carriageway.

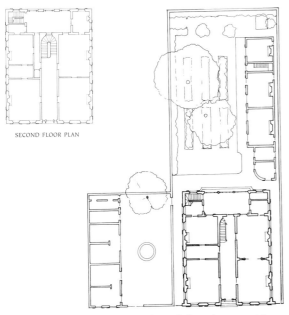

SECOND FLOOR PLAN

RA26 Hermann-Grima House, site plan with floor plan, second floor plan

MW115 Hermann-Grima House, 820 St. Louis Street, 1831, William Brand

LL13 Gallier House, 1132 Royal Street, 1857, James Gallier, Jr.

LL13, RA27 *By the time this house was built both the Creole and the American town house types were well established, and a sophisticated architect such as Gallier felt free to combine and borrow from each. In terms of style, he pushed beyond strict Greek Revival classicism with a gallery making full use of the possibilities of cast iron.*

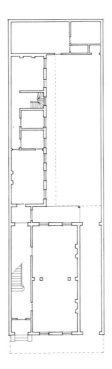
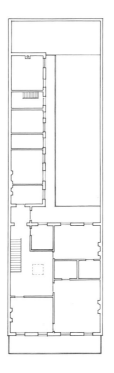

RA27 Gallier House, plans

RA26, MW115 *The large site of this house was originally even larger, extending through the block to Conti Street. The complex included a stable, unusual for the Quarter. Into the house plan, which might otherwise belong to a town house on the Eastern seaboard, are integrated a gallery and cabinets, typical of a Creole house (p. 115). Similarly, a simple balcony is the only local touch on the brick façade, which addresses the street in a forthright American manner. Two carefully-designed Federal doorways are stacked one above the other.*

47

TYPES

K75 location uncertain

K75 Wooden box steps project regularly into French Quarter sidewalks from the faces of shotgun houses. Box-like enclosures to either side of the steps serve as shelves, benches, and footrests for street activities.

SHOTGUN HOUSE
DATES: LATER 1800s AND EARLY 1900s

The basic shotgun house is a long row of rooms marching away from the street in single file. The roof ridge is perpendicular to the street. The name *shotgun* is usually attributed to the notion that, if one wanted to fire a gun through a door in the front, the shot would continue unimpeded through the lined-up doors of each successive room. The explanation doesn't suggest why somebody would want to fire a shotgun through a house. Beyond that, the explanation seems apocryphal. Though lined-up doors can present a handsome sequence with shafts of yellow sunlight coming into the rooms between them, such an enfilade is actually not common; doors of the successive rooms generally do not line up, at least not all of them.

Conjecture also surrounds the origins of the shotgun house. There are a handful of French Quarter cottages one room wide and several rooms deep which survive from the first decades of the nineteenth century (see p. 36). These have been used to support a theory proposed by John Michael Vlach that the New Orleans shotgun house evolved from a house found among the Yoruba people of west Africa, having been transmuted and brought here by refugees from the slave uprisings in the Caribbean in the late eighteenth and early nineteenth centuries.[12] This theory may be plausible in the case of the early cottages. It was decades later however—relatively late in the nineteenth century—when the shotgun as we know it came to be built in large numbers in New Orleans. To think that this movement took its remarkable energy from a fairly uncommon type of cottage built decades earlier seems too much of a stretch.

More likely, the shotgun developed as a relatively inexpensive solution to building separate houses on New Orleans' narrow lots. Builders avidly seized upon the possibility of varying the façades of these houses by using machine-cut wooden decoration. Out of catalogs they concocted amazing façade compositions which still today line block after block of New Orleans streets. Because of their repetitive, speculative construction—and because in the Quarter they replaced older, more hand-wrought structures—shotgun houses were not highly regarded by early preservationists. The longer they have survived, however, the more venerated they have become. Shotguns in rows drum up a lively rhythm of projecting steps, overhangs, and prefabricated decoration which now constitutes an essential part of the Quarter street scene. Sometimes they are set back from the sidewalk with small yards and front galleries, but more often they follow Quarter street etiquette, sitting squarely on the sidewalk with a set of "box steps." On these wooden steps with small bench-like platforms to either side, generations of New Orleanians have practiced "stoop sitting," a social and conversational art.

Inside, shotgun rooms are generally high-ceilinged and not small—fourteen feet square might be a normal size. They may be elaborately detailed, commodious and even elegant by modern standards. In the original layout of rooms the kitchen was the last, opening into a rear yard used for laundry and service. Often (as with other house types) the yard contained a wooden cistern to collect rainwater from the house roof.

Shotguns come in three principal shapes:

THE SINGLE SHOTGUN

THE DOUBLE SHOTGUN

THE CAMELBACK

Each shape has numerous variations, inventively investigated by builders.

K112 1112-16 Bourbon Street, c. 1888, detail

K112 *An overhang on the front of a shotgun house shades the front openings as the abat-vent does the Creole cottage. More often than not, mass-produced wooden brackets punctuate the overhangs. Their purpose is more decorative than structural since the overhangs are usually cantilevered from the roof structure.*

COMFORT, PRIVACY AND THE LACK OF CORRIDORS

A fact of life in the most typical kind of shotgun house is the lack of corridors, thus the necessity of going through one room to reach another. The lack of corridors is also typical of other French Quarter house types including the Creole cottage and often the Creole town house. Architect Benjamin Henry Latrobe and writer Lafcadio Hearn both occupied rented rooms in French Quarter buildings for extended periods during different decades of the nineteenth century. They formed opposite opinions about the need for corridors in New Orleans houses.

We derive from the English the habit of desiring that every one of our rooms should be separately accessible, & we consider rooms that are thoroughfares as useless. The French & Continental Europeans generally live, I believe, as much to their own satisfaction in their houses as we do in ours, & employ the room they have to more advantage because they do not require so much space for passages. The comfort is a matter of habit.

Benjamin Henry Latrobe,
Impressions Respecting New Orleans[13]

The double cottage is an abomination; and even the single cottage without a hallway is an affliction. Is it agreeable to be unable to go to bed either without passing through somebody else's room or having somebody else passing through your room? It is not even a civilized way of living; and certainly a vast majority of New Orleans houses would appear to a stranger to have been constructed with little regard to common decency.

Lafcadio Hearn,
Creole Sketches[14]

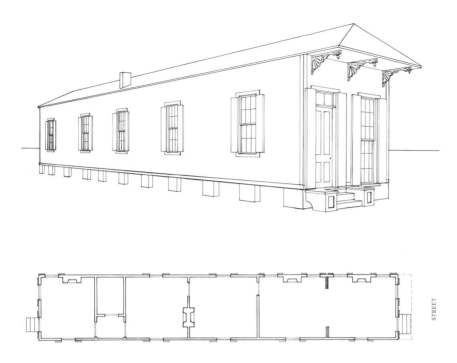

SINGLE SHOTGUN HOUSE

This simplest form of shotgun house is actually less common than the double. A door and a window open to the street or to a small porch. Rooms line up in single file, two sharing a chimney on their common wall. Each room can have openings on either two or three sides, so there can be abundant light and ventilation.

RA28 plan of a typical single shotgun house

STREET

MH63 1300 Chartres Street, c. 1890

MH63, MH56, MH53
Not much wider than boxcars, these three single shotguns fit into unusually narrow spaces, carved out of or left over from wider lots. The Chartres Street house is brick, which is less common than wood. It also has a porch, while the other two abut the sidewalk directly.

MH56 1022 Orleans Street, c. 1880

MH53 1005 St. Philip Street, c. 1896

DOUBLE SHOTGUN HOUSE

This type eliminated the cross-ventilation possible in the single shotgun. But it allowed double densities per lot and became particularly common for speculative construction. It also served the social pattern, common in New Orleans, of including two generations or branches of a family in the same house.

MH83 920-24 Dumaine Street, c. 1890

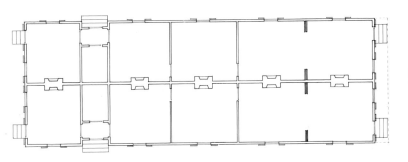

RA29 plan of a typical double shotgun house

MH88 830-32 St. Peter Street, c. 1890

K122 1109-11 Bourbon Street, c. 1890

MH83 *The hipped roof of this double extends over its porch. Raised higher than most such houses, it has a single stair inserted into the porch.*

MH88 *A fence, a small yard, and a porch separate the front wall of this double from the edge of the sidewalk. Such placement, common elsewhere in the city, is rare in the Quarter.*

K122 *Set just at the sidewalk's edge, this house addresses the street in typical shotgun fashion. A much older two-story brick service structure (c. 1824) remains behind it, left from a previous house on the site. Shotguns are relatively recent Quarter buildings and often replaced earlier structures.*

51

TYPES

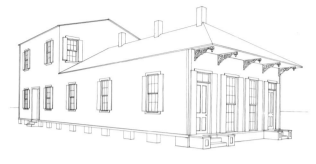

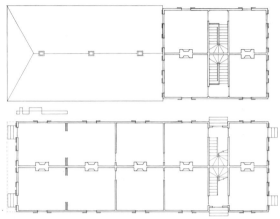

MH55 *Gables of different sizes stack one behind the other, relieving some of the awkwardness inherent in the camelback shape.*

RA plan of a typical shotgun camelback

CAMELBACK AND OTHER VARIANTS

A camelback has a partial second floor, a "hump," placed over the rear of the ground floor. The hump permits stacking one or more rooms onto the shotgun plan, single or double. The stairway, sandwiched between the rear rooms, normally has its own exterior door opening into a side alleyway. Sometimes, still today, a hump is added to enlarge a single-story shotgun.

The shotgun house type has numerous other variations, most of which are developed more elaborately in parts of the city outside the French Quarter. Galleries can be added at the front. A gallery or corridor can be added in an additional bay along the side of the run of rooms. Sometimes such a space is part gallery, part corridor, playing with varying degrees of enclosure. Projecting bays, square or octagonal, can extend perpendicular to the house; sometimes these have their own galleries. Side balconies can be added to upper floors of camelbacks, often serving as exterior circulation. Extra bays added to doubles yield five and six bay examples. One also finds two-story shotguns—not camelbacks because the second story is the same size as the first. These can be found as double or single and are subject to the same variations as single-story shotguns. Finally, these variants move so far from the simple single or double shotgun house that limits of the type begin to blur.

MH55 904-06 Dumaine Street, c. 1899

MH33 1023 Dumaine Street, c. 1880

MH34 813 Barracks Street, c. 1886

MH33, MH34 *Both these houses are variations on the linear shotgun plan. The entrance bay leads first to enclosed space and then to an open side gallery. The Dumaine Street house has also a front gallery and a camelback. On Barracks Street the entrance is recessed.*

MH35 *The two-story single shotgun stacks rooms atop as well as behind each other.*

MH85 *This double has an extra bay, a side gallery, and a two-story wing at the rear with galleries of its own. The two-story section does not extend the full width of the house as a camelback normally does.*

MH35 811 Barracks Street, c. 1900

MH85 823-25 Burgundy Street, c. 1890

COMPONENTS OF FRENCH QUARTER BUILDINGS

If you were kidnapped in some distant airport, blindfolded, brought to the French Quarter and locked inside a typical structure, chances are you could tell where you were by recognizing a few components. One finds the same components used over and over in different types of buildings and in different styles of architecture. They can be imagined as a kit of parts from which these buildings were made. Most buildings will have some of these parts, some may have all of them.

That so many of these components control the effects of light, air and heat is revealing. The responses of these buildings to climate—and the synthesis of these responses with the city's centuries of cultural mixing—comprise a quite specific response to place, the stuff of a regional architecture.

Many of the components of New Orleans buildings are designed to respond to a particular sub-tropical climate that does not permit itself to be ignored. Travellers' accounts usually refer to it. English visitor Harriet Martineau described how the heat affected, not just the feel, but the *look* of things in 1837.

...everything seemed to tell us that we had plunged into the dogdays. I never knew before how impressions of heat can be conveyed through the eye. The intensity of glare and shadow in the streets, and the many evidences that the fear of heat is the prevailing idea of the place, affect the imagination even more than the scorching power of the sun does the bodily frame.

Harriet Martineau, "The Haunted House," from *The World from Jackson Square*[1]

RK26 Napoleon House, 500 Chartres Street

MW114 Hermann-Grima House, 820 St. Louis Street

RK3 234-40 Bourbon Street

RH705 705 Toulouse Street

DOORS AND DOORWAYS
Pictured on these pages is a compendium of basic door types. Within types, of course, the variations of size and style are endless. French Quarter buildings often use doors or pairs of doors where one might expect windows. Doors usually have larger openings than windows and allow a greater air flow.

The doors have been organized within the following categories:

ENTRANCE DOORWAYS

CARRIAGEWAY DOORS

CASEMENT DOORS

SINGLE DOORS

MULTIPLE DOORS

K194A 908 St. Louis Street

RK20 436-40 Chartres Street

ENTRANCE DOORWAYS

Entrance doorways are part of a building's public identity. This seems to have been less important for Creoles than for Americans. The entrance to an American town house is usually larger and more imposing than the building's other doors. But in the Creole town house the residential use is shared with a commercial one, and the size of the carriageway or passage door is more a matter of use than rhetoric.

CL23 619-21 Esplanade Avenue

RK26, RK3, RH705, MW114, K194A, RK20 *Except for the door to the passage at the Napoleon House, all of these entrance doors have arched heads. Arches, either segmental, elliptical or round were a common feature of French Quarter buildings from French Colonial times through the first decades of the nineteenth century. All these openings were built prior to 1835.*

RK95B 1016 St. Louis Street

K192 1025 St. Louis Street

MH13 840 Conti Street

K126B 1303 Bourbon Street

CL23, RK95B, K192, MH13, K126B *Around 1835, interest grew in the architectural forms of ancient Greece. Flat openings came to be favored over arched ones. Columns and entablatures were often used for the vertical and horizontal members needed to frame and give importance to entrance doorways. On many buildings, openings that had been built as arches were modified to reflect the new preference for rectangles.*

CARRIAGEWAY DOORS
The Creole town house usually has no such thing as a back door. The carriageway door (or, in smaller houses, the passage door) had to work for both individual entries and deliveries, for both people and vehicles.

MW155 *Carriageway doors serve individual users as well as vehicles. A three-panel arrangement such as this allows the center leaf to open easily. The barred transom provides security while allowing a generous passage of air.*

MW155 address uncertain

RK109C *The carriageway door into a building with an entresol looks simpler than it is. The horizontal member at the springpoint of the arch actually represents the floor line of the entresol. The lower doors, undoubtedly replacements, are fabricated with pieces of lath spaced to allow light and and air into the carriageway. A smaller doorway for individual passage is set within one leaf.*

RH821 *The transom at this carriageway is glazed, with a radial pattern of muntins. The central of the three leaves opens independently of the others.*

RK109C 514 Toulouse Street

RH821 Royal Street

RKm14 Nicolas house, 723 Toulouse Street

K163 715 Gov. Nicholls Street

RK45 1012-14 Dauphine Street

MH15 624 Pirates' Alley

CASEMENT DOORS
Casement doors, or French doors, allow light to enter and, when open, do not protrude as deeply into rooms as single doors. Normally found in exterior openings, they are also used for interior doors when there is a need to pass light from one room to another, They were favored by Creole builders; Americans preferred single doors.

RKm14 These tall, slender doors are from a house built in 1808. Each leaf has fourteen lights.

K163 A transom moderates the height of these doors. Security comes not from the doors but from the batten shutters which close to protect them.

RK45 Casement doors sit next to a single door which opens to a passage through the center of this cottage. Both openings have arched heads and barred transoms. Shutters are eliminated at the single door.

MH15 A plaid muntin design organizes the panes of glass in these doors. Shutters protect the doors but not the semi-circular transom. These doors are part of a series of similar openings on the eleven Labranche buildings.

K23 1034 Chartres Street, detail

SINGLE DOORS
Single doors have a wide
varety of panel sizes and
configurations. If the door
has no transom, it may
need to be extra tall so that
the top of its frame aligns
with those of windows in
the same room.

RK43 Gardette-LePrêtre house, 716 Dauphine Street

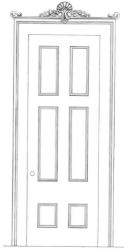

RA30 Gauche house, 704 Esplanade Avenue

RH820C Hermann-Grima House, 820 St. Louis Street

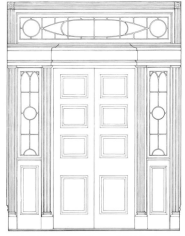

RA31 Beauregard House, 1113 Chartres Street

MH38 1227 Chartres Street

MULTIPLE DOORS

For wider openings solutions range from simple double doors, to sliding doors which pocket into walls, to doors hinged to fold back. Though some solutions are repeated many times, builders were willing to innovate when the opportunity arose.

61

L5 Madame John's Legacy, 628-32 Dumaine Street

WINDOWS

The windows of French Quarter buildings are mostly large and loose, allowing abundant light and the flushing of rooms with air. Windows usually work in conjunction with shutters which expand the number of conditions possible—light without air, air with little light, regulated amounts of light and air, complete openness, or complete closure.

RA32 Pedesclaux-Le Monnier house, 636-40 Royal Street

RKm30 Bosque house, 617-19 Chartres Street

L5 *The segmentally-arched head and small panes of these casements identify them with the French Colonial style. These retain their old hand-wrought hardware, including the characteristic "mustache" hinges.*

RA32 *With its asymmetrical shape and sliding sash, this loggia window accommodates the angle of a stairway.*

RKm30 *Casements with fan-shaped transoms were commonly used in loggias.*

CASEMENT WINDOWS
Casement windows make sense for a hot climate because they allow the entire window to open, whereas double-hung windows block air movement with their stacked sashes.

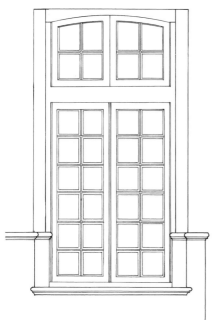

RA33 casement with transom, Ursuline Convent, 1100-16 Chartres Street

MH47 823-25 Bourbon Street

RK29 Napoleon House, 500 Chartres Street

RA33, MH47 *Both of these windows are divided into casements below and transoms above. The styles of the transoms distinguish the French Colonial windows of the Ursuline Convent from the Federal style ones on the Creole cottage. The cottage's casement windows match its casement doors.*

RK29 *Casements work in conjunction with shutters. Together, the two permit the change of mood in a room by the control of light and air.*

K216 902 Toulouse Street

K216 *Projecting shop windows called* vitrines *came into use in the second half of the nineteenth century. Openings in existing buildings were often modified to accommodate them.*

K90 202 Bourbon Street

DOUBLE- AND TRIPLE-HUNG WINDOWS

With the Americans came double- and triple-hung windows. Over time they were mixed freely with other windows and doors—a Creole cottage may have double-hung windows next to casement doors. Triple-hung windows became an alternative to casement doors. Their higher openings allow windows to be used for access to balconies.

K90 *Casement doors, several shapes of double-hungs, and even the horizontal frieze windows popular in Greek Revival buildings are put together in one town house.*

HC16, RA34 *Twelve-over-twelve windows were used on the sides of the Beauregard House which has casement doors across the front.*

HC16 Beauregard House, 1113 Chartres Street, detail

MH40 1227 Chartres Street

MH45 823-25 Bourbon Street

MH45 *A six-over-six arrangement of panes became common in the nineteenth century.*

MH40 *When completely open, triple-hung windows allow passage to a balcony.*

MH39 *In an unusual variation on the triple-hung window, the bottom "sash" is a wooden panel.*

K176 *A slip-head window is used on this Italianate façade to allow the same openness achieved by the triple-hung window. The taller bottom sash slides up into a pocket above the upper sash.*

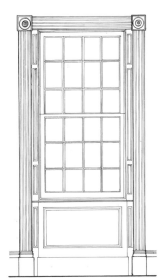

RA34 Interior of double-hung window, Beauregard House

MH39 604 Esplanade Avenue

K176 819 Orleans Street

RA35 transom, Beauregard House

RA36 transom, Ursuline Convent

RH1113 interior doors, Beauregard House, 1101-13 Chartres Street

TRANSOMS

Transoms serve functional purposes—they admit light and, if opened, air. In visual terms they bring the height of a door up to the height of a tall window so the openings in a given room can align at the top. And the design of their sometimes elaborate muntins provided a place for a builder to lend distinction to his structure. Transoms at the Beauregard House and at 527-33 Royal Street (the Merieult house, now the Historic New Orleans Collection) give an idea of the graceful and ingenious geometries that are possible.

Round-headed and elliptical openings presented special opportunities for the development of fan transoms. Transoms in carriageways were left open, with iron bars or louvers fitted in for security.

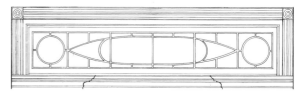

RA37 front door transom, Beauregard House

MW66 central door at the rear of the Ursuline Convent, 1100 Chartres Street

K26 elliptical louvered transom, 1121 Chartres Street

66

RH628A fan transoms, rear of 628 Toulouse Street

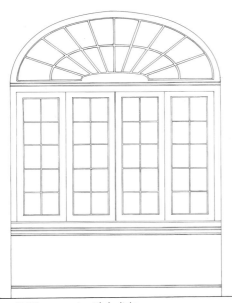

RA38 casements with fanlight

MH14 *trompe l'oeil* transom, 841 Royal Street

LL35A 527-33 Royal Street

RH527B 527-33 Royal Street

67

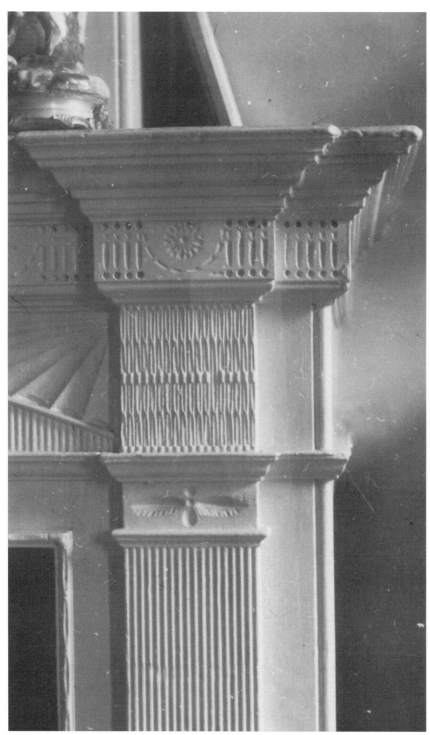

RK113N Nicolas house, 723 Toulouse Street

MANTELS

The most characteristic French Quarter mantel is the box mantel of the Creole builders. The chimney projects into the rooms and the mantelshelf wraps three sides of it. The "box" below the mantelshelf may extend out nearly to the edges of the shelf, which sometimes forms a kind of cornice for pilasters at either side of the fireplace. The front and sides of the mantel as well as the overmantel may be carved and decorated. Decorations may tie in with plaster moldings around the ceiling, so that the mantel is linked into a system with door and window openings. Together they can form a coherent interior architecture-of-the-room, an integrated layer of spatial punctuations and emphases which project from the surface of the walls.

RK113G 723 Toulouse Street

RK50C 612 Dumaine Street

RK50B 612 Dumaine Street

RK50A 612 Dumaine Street

RK113N, RK113G *Reeding and gouge work make the surface of this mantel rich with shadow. The mantel is in a house built in 1808, during a time when New Orleans Francophiles were enthusiastic about Napoleon. The winged figure, if we interpret it as a bee, may reflect that enthusiasm, as Napoleon used a bee as his emblem. But it looks more like a leaf with berries, which is probably what the carver had in mind.*

RK50C, RK50B, RK50A *Mantel decoration often relies on the elements of classical architecture—pilasters with bases and capitals supporting an entablature which run along above. Here lower pilasters support more pilasters on the overmantel. The finely-carved central piece looks almost like a floating pilaster capital, most of its shaft having been amputated by the opening.*

69

RK90C, RK90B *The shelf swells at the center of this mantel from a Creole cottage of 1824. Reeding, the small convex molding cut into the wood, decorates the central block as well as a small ellipse over the capital of the thin column at the mantel's end.*

MH42 *Ionic columns of black marble support an entablature and mantelshelf. The mantel is in the parlor of a Creole town house of about 1830.*

RH1014C *This straightforward wooden mantel is from a Creole town house built in 1827.*

RK90C Gaillard cottage, 915-17 St. Ann Street

RK90B Gaillard cottage, 915-17 St. Ann Street

MH42 1227 Chartres Street

RH1014C 1014 Chartres Street

MISCELLANEOUS HARDWARE

Before the mass manufacture of hardware, French Quarter blacksmiths forged a range of functional and decorative hinges and latches from iron and other metals. Drawings shown here were made for the Historic American Buildings Survey, most of them during the 1930s when architect Richard Koch directed the Louisiana division. Young "delineators" working on the project at that time included architect and historian Samuel Wilson, Jr., and artist Boyd Cruise, who became the first director of the Historic New Orleans Collection.

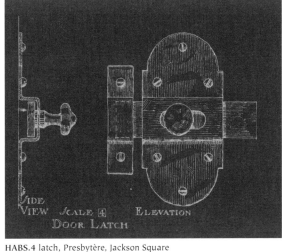

HABS.4 latch, Presbytère, Jackson Square

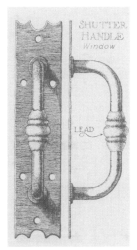

HABS.7 shutter handle, 1218-20 Burgundy Street

RH1014A thumb latch, 1014 Chartres Street

HABS.9 latch, 1218-20 Burgundy Street

HABS.6 bottom bolt

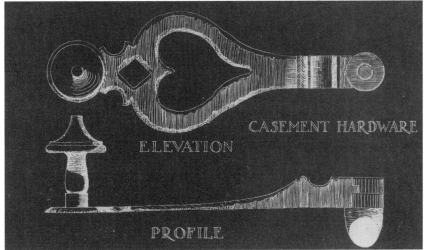

HABS.2 casement hardware, Cabildo, Jackson Square

CL24 *Shutters can be solid, can be louvered, or can be some combination of the two. Solid shutters are called batten shutters. This Clarence Laughlin photograph shows a variety of shutter types accommodated on one corner of a façade.*

RK14 819 Burgundy

RK14 *Between a handsome pair of paneled shutters, a wooden gate keeps small children and pets inside.*

SHUTTERS

French Quarter shutters are a physical diagram of the subtle balances builders have established between the separate demands of security, light and air. Ingenious in their own design, they are also capable of "dressing" a façade, giving it varying patterns depending on which ones are open or closed, and transferring shadow patterns to the spaces inside.

RK98B 726 St. Peter Street

RK98B *Batten shutters, when closed, make the rooms inside quite dark. Diamond shaped openings are a traditional device for allowing some light to enter.*

MH16 Napoleon House,
500 Chartres Street

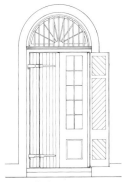

RA39 break shutter

K174 717 Orleans Street

RA39 *Some shutters, called break shutters, are designed to fold in the center of a leaf. In their closed position they are recessed from the building surface, and in their open position they bend to lie flat against the wall.*

K174 *Now a hotel, this building was a convent for the Sisters of the Holy Family at the time of this photograph. The louvered screen on the balcony provided privacy for the nuns.*

73

MW112 Court of the Two Lions, 700-710 Toulouse Street

K205 *Rails in the shutters align with those of the casement doors they protect. The shutters are panelled below the rail and louvered above it.*

MH12 *Fixed louvers are used on this eighteenth-century portion of the Napoleon House. Larger, fixed louvers preceded smaller, adjustable blades.*

K205 1008-10 St. Peter Street

MH12 Napoleon House, 535-37 St. Louis Street

MW112 *Shuttered balconies were not uncommon, especially on service structures, since balconies often served as circulation paths for members of a household. Here panels within the screens open like casement windows, adding another degree of choice to the matter of light, privacy, air movement and view. They clearly allowed the hanging out of clothes as well, a light-catching motif in many of the photographs of Morgan Whitney.*

MW151, address uncertain

K139 825 Chartres Street, detail

K139 *Somewhat wider than usual, these shutters have leaves divided into two panels of louvers. Shutters on the box balconies above cannot open flat against the wall and must assume a position like fins protruding from the wall surface.*

K53C 713-19 Royal Street

MW151 *Louvered shutters permit ventilation and light for the rooms inside but are less secure against intrusion. In such a building as this, batten shutters are used at the street level where strength is most needed. Diamond-shaped openings placed above eye level allow a little light into the ground-floor rooms when the shutters are closed. Note how the positions of the shutters play with the shadow cast by the balcony.*

K53C *This photograph shows that at some point the shutters of the Vignie houses had panels of glass installed in them. For whatever reason the glazing occurred, it gives the effect of out-swinging casements or even storm windows and adds an odd reflectivity to this otherwise free-breathing 1830s townhouse row.*

RK4 234-40 Bourbon Street

MH4 *These double parlors are joined by tall double doors and illuminated by tall windows at either end. A loggia and stairway are visible through the windows at the rear of the photograph.*

RK4 *A stairway winds through the upper zone of this arcaded space.*

MH4 604 Esplanade Avenue

TALL ROOMS

Ordinary rooms in ordinary French Quarter buildings have ceilings that range from 11 to 14 feet high. Even in the smaller service structures behind the larger buildings, the ceilings are only a foot or two lower. A principal reason is coolness; there is an upper zone in each room where the hottest air collects above the heads of the occupants. But the generosity of that upper zone also has a haptic dimension. People stand taller in high spaces. Tall rooms are part of the Quarter paradox of abundant space within a tight network of buildings.

MW41 St. Louis Hotel, 600 St. Louis Street, built 1835; re-built after fire, 1840; J.N.B. and J.I. DePouilly, demolished 1916

Morgan Whitney made a series of photographs of the interior of the St. Louis Hotel prior to its demolition. The tall spaces, the decrepitude, and the memory of the major slave exchange which it housed before the Civil War were described by British novelist John Galsworthy. He visited the empty hotel in 1912 when it must have been in a more advanced state of decay than the photographs show. He mentioned "the crumbling black and white marble floorings" and "the water… trickling into pools. And down in the halls there came to us wandering—strangest thing that ever strayed through deserted grandeur—a brown, broken horse, lean, with a sore flank and a head of tremendous age. It stopped and gazed at us, as though we might be going to give it things to eat, and then passed on, stumbling over the ruined marbles."

"That Old-time Place,"
The Inn of Tranquility
1912

MW40 St. Louis Hotel

MW42 St. Louis Hotel

MW41, MW40, MW42 *The columned space was evidently the hotel lobby, of which the slave auction platform was a part. The hotel included a copper-covered dome built using a system of hollow terra cotta cylinders. The lower photographs seem to be of spaces beneath the dome. See page 76 for Whitney's photograph of the hotel stairway.*

MW45 St. Louis Hotel, 600 St. Louis Street, built 1835; re-built after fire, 1840; J.N.B. and J.I. DePouilly, demolished 1916

MW45 *Among the photographs Morgan Whitney made of he interior of the St. Louis Hotel was this one of its staircase. Beginning on a raised platform, it spiraled around a chandelier and rose into an octagonal opening.*

STAIRWAYS
The French Quarter's oldest stairway actually predates its oldest building. The stairway which still survives in the Ursuline Convent of 1750 was probably removed and reused from the first convent structure, built in 1734. Since then richly varied stairways, mostly crafted of wood, have been devised and built for the Quarter's public and private structures.

RK5 234-40 Bourbon Street

MW87 Brulatour Courtyard, 516-22 Royal Street

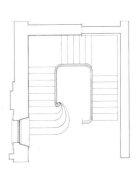

RKm26 Pedesclaux-Le Monnier house, 636-40 Royal Street

RH624 624 Royal Street

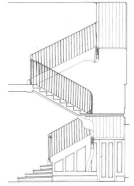

RA40 plan and elevation, Ursuline Convent stair, probably 1734

79

RH628 628 Royal Street

RH723A 723 Toulouse Street

RKm27.2 709-13 Bourbon Street

RK27 Napoleon House, 500 Chartres Street

BB1 Cabildo, detail, Jackson Square

Stairways suggest motion. They introduce diagonal lines into static architectural compositions. Light filters down and up their walls in ways that stimulate photographers to compose them within two-dimensional frames.

Safety codes in the twentieth century require that stairs be straight and wide and not very steep. The architects and builders of these French Quarter stairways suffered fewer

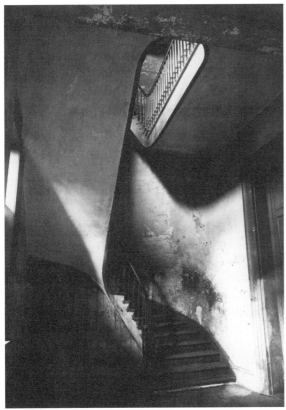

RH828 Olivier house, 828-30 Toulouse Street

restraints, but had nevertheless to negotiate a complex set of requirements. They must begin and end at positions that work with the building's plan and its structure. They need natural illumination. Railings must correspond with the often irregular ascent of the stair risers. When they do all these things and achieve a certain grace as well, they deserve the attention these photographers have given them.

CL25 830 Royal Street

MW88 837-39 Royal Street

MW88, MW89 *Balconies wrap two sides of this courtyard, shown in two photographs by Morgan Whitney. The lattice screening provides a measure of privacy for these narrow outdoor spaces which communicate between various rooms of the house. Across the dividing wall between the two properties (a pair of Royal Street town houses) the adjacent service structure is almost a mirror image.*

MW89 837-39, 841 Royal Street

BALCONIES & GALLERIES

As the term is used in the French Quarter, a balcony is a narrow (three or four foot) projection from the wall of a building, not supported by columns from the ground. A gallery is wider (normally the width of the sidewalk) and because of its greater width, requires support from columns, usually iron, sometimes wooden. Balconies may face either a street or a courtyard; galleries more often hang over the street. A more conventional porch is also called a gallery.

Balconies on the courtyard side serve as outdoor corridors, connecting the rooms of the main house with the smaller rooms of the service wing. When balconies and galleries appear on the street side, they take on a public dimension; standing on a gallery, looking over a rail and framed by cast iron filigree, one is conscious both of seeing and being seen. One senses not only the less-privileged mortals moving below but also the series of other balconies at one's own level, a community of which one is not really aware from the ground. As in other aspects of the Quarter, a theatrical analogy suggests itself: the occupant of a gallery sits in a loge. At Mardi Gras the dialog between balcony and street (or loge and stage) becomes loud and bawdy, and may reverse itself; strings of beads (and glimpses of body parts) pass back and forth, and balconies become stages.

Hypothesizing about the origins of the New Orleans gallery has been an irresistible game. Jay Edwards points logically to the West Indies as the inspiration for the addition of galleries to the otherwise-cold-weather buildings constructed by the early French colonists.[2] Once introduced and from whatever source, these partially enclosed, partially open spaces had undeniable value. They became an element on which builders could innovate and play variations; they join the range of "in-between spaces" that are perhaps the

MW94 location uncertain

most characteristic elements of French Quarter architecture—loggias, carriageways, passages, balconies, galleries, distinguished from each other by different sizes and degrees of enclosure. Of these, the sidewalk-wide gallery with an ornamental frame of cast iron is only the most obvious.

Balconies and galleries work both as space and as overhang. They extend inside rooms out beyond their walls, providing a sunny, more airy realm. They are a spatial baffle between *room* and *outdoors*. They can be roofed or not. Either way they protect windows and doors below them from direct sun and rain, allowing them to be left open during a summer shower. Even after decades of air conditioning (and as respite from the resulting claustrophobia) many Quarter residents seek as much occasion as possible to open up their rooms to light and air.

MW94 Primitive plumbing seems to have been added to the loggia to which this louvered balcony attaches; perhaps a sink is mounted inside beneath the altered window. At the time of the photograph, probably between 1890 and 1910, changes in plumbing and notions of convenience were affecting the balconies and loggias of these buildings. The dress of the figures silhouetted in the carriageway helps corroborate the date.

M29 gallery on the rear of the Ursuline Convent, now removed, 1100 Chartres Street

M29, MW63 *Ernest J. Bellocq's photograph registers a tactile awareness of the materials of the Ursuline Convent, brought close by the gallery which allowed one to be next to the upper walls. The gallery, not original, was once attached to the river side of the Convent and has since been removed. A plain affair of turned wooden posts and a wooden railing, its ceiling hits the Convent walls abruptly, obscuring the top of the stucco arch over the central door. Nevertheless, as the photograph shows, it was a generous gallery, one scaled more to a plantation house than to a city structure. The Morgan Whitney photograph from some time around the turn of the century shows the external appearance.*

MW63 Ursuline Convent, rear view showing gallery, now removed

LL32A Pontalba Buildings, Jackson Square

K60B 615 Royal Street

K44 901 Gov. Nicholls Street

K41 628 Gov. Nicholls Street (note screens)

LL32A *The Pontalba buildings exemplify the local distinction made between* balcony *and* gallery. *The balcony, on the third floor, is relatively narrow and cantilevered from the side of the building. The gallery, on the second floor, covers the width of the sidewalk below and is supported on posts.*

K60B *Among balconies, a distinction is made between* box balconies *and the usual* continuous balconies. *On the façades of these town houses the box balconies are at the third floor, above the continuous balconies at the second. Box balconies expand slightly the space of the room inside and give their occupant a feeling of importance. Continuous balconies are more communal and communicative.*

K44 *The original balcony on this corner building was replaced by a gallery in the last quarter of the nineteenth century. Built around 1840 as one of a pair of American town houses, the building evolved to include a store with a corner entrance. Such an evolution, especially the construction of a gallery, happened all over the Quarter after 1850—balconies with wrought iron railings gave way to galleries framed with cast iron.*

K41 *The French Quarter participated in the era of the screen porch, with the occasional screening of galleries. Mosquitoes, currently reduced to reasonable numbers by spraying trucks, have traditionally represented a substantial local population.*

K62 1004-06 Royal

K35 810-12 Dumaine Street

MH48 714 Gov. Nicholls Street

K62, K35, MH48 *Balconies of service buildings usually have wooden posts and railings, whereas iron supports and railing are more usual on street-front balconies.*

K179 *A cottage of one-and-one-half floors has no place for balconies on its front or back, but can have them applied to its gable ends. Since the house is on a corner, this balcony gives the side of the building something of a public mien.*

K179 738-40 Orleans Street (seen from the Bourbon Street side)

K74 841 Ursulines Street

K74, K146 *Galleries sit on these buildings a bit like eyeglasses or other prosthetic devices—not physically integrated with them, but essential to the way they work. The Ursulines Street house is thought to have grown from one to two stories around 1873 and the gallery was probably added then. The wondrous galleries on the Gardette-LePrêtre house, so high above the ground and so compressed on the top level, were alterations made decades after the 1836 construction date.*

K146 Gardette-LePrêtre house, 716 Dauphine Street

K66 location uncertain

K66 *Cast iron railings and supports enframe the second story gallery of this town house, but wrought iron was used on the third which is unroofed. Pretty much any imaginable combination of materials and configurations can be found, since ironwork has been used and removed and re-used as buildings and needs have come and gone.*

RK108 1023 St. Philip Street

RK108, RKm29, RK102F
Sometimes an abat-vent *is a separate piece of roof, supported by projecting iron bars and covered with sheet metal, as at 1023 St. Philip Street or on the Ursulines Street cottage. Other times, as at 827 St. Philip Street, it is a simple extension of wooden roof members, causing the roof to have a double pitch.*

MH64 *An uneven succession of abat-vents and balconies dance up and down along the street.*

MH64 728 & 732 Gov. Nicholls Street

RKm29 1026 Ursulines Street, demolished

ABAT-VENTS

Abat-vents are overhanging roofs usually found on the street fronts of low houses and commercial structures, especially Creole cottages. An abat-vent may be a direct extension of a wooden roof structure or a sloping plane of sheet metal separately supported on projecting iron bars. Like balconies and galleries, *abat-vents* give shade and rain protection to whatever lies below them. At the scale of a street, the succession of *abat-vents* not only provides a sheltered walkway but also energizes street elevations. A row of them along the street will jump up and down, together with balconies and galleries, to follow the varying floor heights of buildings.

ABAT-VENTS—*A PUBLIC AMENITY*

An *abat-vents* extends a piece of a house over the sidewalk. It borrows a bit of public space to protect its walls and windows and doors. In return it gives a measure of protection to the pedestrian. Describing a remote street of the Quarter, Benjamin Henry Latrobe wrote of the usefulness of this *quid pro quo.*

The roofs are high, covered with tiles or shingles, & project five feet over the footway, which is also five feet wide. The eaves therefore discharge the water into the gutters. The highth [sic] of the stories is hardly ten feet, the elevation above the pavement not more than a foot & a half; & therefore the eaves are not often more than 8 feet from the ground. However different this mode is from the American manner of building, it has very great advantages both with regard to the interior of the dwelling & to the street. In the summer the walls are perfectly shaded from the sun & the house kept cool, while the passengers are also shaded from the sun & protected from the rain. From my lodgings to Mr. Nolte's is a distance [of] 650 feet independently of the crossing of two streets, & yet in the heaviest rains I can walk to his house perfectly dry excepting for about 200 feet in front of a dead Wall & some high houses in Thoulouse [sic] street.

> Benjamin Henry Latrobe
> *Impressions Respecting New Orleans*
> Diary & Sketches, 1818-1820[3]

RK102F 827-29 St. Philip Street

RH500C Napoleon house, 500 Chartres Street, detail

RH401 Louisiana State Bank, 401-03 Royal Street, detail

RH401 *This dormer sits atop a bank structure designed by distinguished American architect Benjamin Henry Latrobe. With its good proportion and such careful details as the semi-circular louvered transom, one assumes it to be an original part of its building. Beneath the present roof, however, is a low-pitched roof which must pre-date the present roof and its dormers. This dormer, with its round top repeating the arched openings on the building's façades, is evidently a sympathetic addition by a later designer.*

RH500C *The Napoleon House is first recognized by the octagonal cupola on its roof, source of some of the tales attached to the building ("built to watch for the arrival of Napoleon's ship," etc., etc.). Dormers also look out from several positions on the roof. The upper sashes of the tall dormers are divided into twelve glass panes of various shapes. Muntins of delicate curvature hold in place the six panes of the semi-circular top.*

DORMERS

Sloped roofs are useful for shedding water, and the attic space their shape creates is useful for habitation and storage. Dormers are a good way to get light and air to that space. Little aedicules perched on sloping roofs, they have appeared on French Quarter buildings since French Colonial times. Early ones were likely to be small, but over the decades they grew and changed form, occasionally becoming room-like and even developing porches of their own.

RK97 723 St. Peter Street. detail

RK97 *In company with the gabled roof and the abat-vent, the dormer identifies this building as a Creole cottage of the larger, one-and-one-half-story kind. Here radial muntins divide the arched upper sash.*

M1 741 Ursulines Street, seen from Bourbon Street, detail

M1 *Like body parts elsewhere on Bourbon Street, these dormers have been enlarged. Now almost room-size, they are connected by a balcony.*

L3, RA41, MH8 *Earlier buildings, in general, have smaller dormers. The Gally house dormer of 1830 is both larger and more elaborate than those of the Ursuline Convent and Madame John's Legacy.*

L3 Madame John's Legacy 628–32 Dumaine Street

RA41 Gally houses, 536–40 Chartres Street

MH8 Ursuline Convent, detail, 1100 Chartres Street

91

K189A 733-37 St. Ann Street

K178 926-28 Orleans

K189A *Rarely does a dormer have a gallery to open onto. But this post-supported wooden gallery, propped in place well after the construction of the cottage, provides an extension of the upper floor rooms. The dormer windows have assumed the role of doors. One even sports a pair of round-headed shutters.*

K178 *A sort of reverse dormer, a dormer turned inside-out, this situation probably occurred when a normal dormer was lost to fire or decrepitude.*

RK81B, K195 *Dormer windows with the upper sash arched are common throughout the Quarter. Panes are shaped in many configurations to accommodate the round top.*

RK81B 624 Royal Street

K195 827 St. Louis Street

RH633 633 Dauphine Street

IRONWORK

Like ornamented cages stacked over sidewalks, galleries framed with ironwork line the streets of the French Quarter. Ironwork leans against and attaches itself to building walls, establishing an intermediary zone between building and street. Born of a local taste for the arabesque, ironwork adds an airy quality to the otherwise earthbound streetscape. Like louvered shutters, it suggests by its very openness the movement of air. Ironwork is made in two ways—hand wrought and cast.

K215 720-22 Toulouse Street, detail

RH633 *Wrought iron monograms displaying the initials of a building owner were used in the late eighteenth and early nineteenth centuries. This monogram sits directly beneath a masonic symbol worked into the design.*

K215 *Bold S brackets help support the cantilevered balcony on this Spanish Colonial building.*

93

ARH9 713-715 Gov. Nicholls Street

ARH9 If you follow the lines in this panel and think of each line as a bent and attenuated piece of iron, a certain structure becomes clear. The rectangular elements at the lower left and right are continuous, joining each other across the central mound. Most of the rest are energetic spirals or C-shapes joined together. In the center are circles and ovals, the large central one containing two hearts and a couple of S-shapes. This panel is from a railing of a house built in 1834. The ironwork is similar to other work by Marcellino Hernandez who left at the end of the Spanish Colonial period. It is speculated that he made the railing and that it was removed from an earlier house and installed here.

WROUGHT IRON

The Quarter's earliest ironwork was wrought by hand. The craftsmen were both white and black, and the blacks included both slaves and free men of color.[4] The most celebrated hand wrought decorative iron work dates from the late Spanish Colonial period. Subtle arrangements of ovals, C's and S's, their ends attenuated like calligraphy, decorate the Presbytère, the Cabildo, and a few fine residences of the 1790s. Sometimes a wrought-iron monogram was incorporated into the railings of private residences. More geometric patterns came in with the new century and the ascendency of French and American taste as Spanish domination ended. The names of a few skilled ironworkers survive. Marcellino Hernandez, a native of the Canary Islands, made the railings on the Cabildo and the Orue-Pontalba house across the street (600 St. Peter Street). William Malus is credited with the railings and consoles on the Napoleon House (500 Chartres Street), among others. The handsomely wrought spear points of the fence that surrounds the Old U.S. Mint (400 Esplanade Avenue) are the work of Daniel Dana.

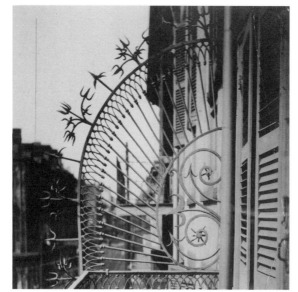

M14 500 block of Royal Street

M14, RKm7 Garde de frise is the French term used for such barriers as these, placed between adjacent balconies. Their intentions are both decorative and menacing.

RH1014B The design of this common railing is called the Cathedral pattern because of its pointed arches. The railing was especially popular in the 1830s.

RKm7 Chartres Street

RH 1014B 1014 Chartres Street, detail

RT11 Cabildo, Jackson Square, detail

RH500B Napoleon House, 500 Chartres Street

RT11, RH500B *Marcellino Hernandez is known to have crafted the wrought iron railings of the Cabildo and the Orue-Pontalba house across the street from it. William Malus is believed to have been responsible for the Napoleon House ironwork. The supporting bracket beneath the balcony is called a* console.

MH69 U.S. Mint, 400 Esplanade Avenue

RKm3B *The flourish of curves at the top of this gate rises to fill the arched portion of the opening which the gate secures.*

MH69 *A line of wrought-iron spear points surrounds the entire block occupied by the U.S. Mint. Daniel Dana was the craftsman responsible for this fence.*

RKm3B 417-25 Royal Street

TF1 Upper Pontalba Buildings, Jackson Square

RH716 Gardette-LePrêtre house, 716 Dauphine Street, 1836

RH716 *Iron posts eighteen feet tall support two levels of galleries which were added to this house years after its construction in 1836. The house's impact on the street must have jumped several fold. The different heights of the two upper floors extend the ironwork in one case and compress it in the other.*

TF1 *The letters A and P combine in this monogram which is recurrent in the ironwork of the Pontalba Buildings. They represent the family name, Almonester, and the married name, Pontalba of the Baroness Pontalba who conceived the buildings and had them constructed.*

CAST IRON

Long used in conjunction with wrought iron for balcony rails, cast iron came into enormous popularity after 1850 when the Baroness Pontalba installed the cast gallery and balcony railings of the Pontalba Buildings at Jackson Square. All over the Quarter building owners replaced their wooden and wrought-iron railings with the new cast iron, frequently enlarging their balconies into post-supported galleries extending the full width of the sidewalk. The transformation of Quarter streets with filigree in the decades after 1850 must have been dramatic. This product of industrialization fed the continuing local taste for florid ornament, evident earlier in Marcellino Hernandez's wrought railings. The Pontalba ironwork of 1850 was manufactured in New York, while the cast-iron fencing which still surrounds Jackson Square is the work of the

RKm24 gallery, Gardette-LePrêtre house

Pelanne Brothers of New Orleans in 1851. A number of local foundries produced not only ornamental railings but also columns, column capitals and entire cast iron façades. Of a handful of surviving cast iron façades in New Orleans, one is at the edge of the Quarter at 111 Exchange Place, designed in 1866 for a commercial structure by architects Gallier and Esterbrook and cast probably by Bennett & Lurges, a local firm.[5] The façade of 521 Royal Street is cast iron at the ground level, with iron trim and a massive iron cornice above.

RKm24 Bracketed by cast-iron, the views from this third floor gallery Gardette-LePrêtre house pass over most French Quarter rooftops to more distant objects. The ironwork provides only a tenuous enclosure, allowing light to reprint its patterns on the floor and air to move freely in and out.

MH65 915 Royal Street

MH65 *This detail belongs to a cast iron ensemble unusual for the stalks and ears of corn it represents. Although the pattern can be found in two other fences in New Orleans, this is its only appearance in the French Quarter.*

LL27 730 Esplanade Avenue

LL27 *This lyre appears as one segment of a cast iron gate opening into a garden from Esplanade Avenue.*

RKm1 cast iron ornament from the gateway to Jackson Square

RKm1, RK70 *The Pelanne brothers of New Orleans used Greek Revival motifs such as the anthemion in the fences and gateways they cast for Jackson Square. The fences, installed in 1851, were part of a general sprucing up of the Square in conjunction with the completion of the Pontalba Buildings. The cast iron benches curve, following the lines of the walks and planting beds laid out at the same time.*

RK70 bench, Jackson Square, detail

K36 917 Dumaine Street

K36 *Built of iron and wood and visually defined with cast iron open work, these balconies and others like them suggest a partly dematerialized volume attached to the face of a quite solid town house. Evidence that the balconies are not in fact dematerialized includes the buckled post supporting them and the shadows they cast.*

The Gauche house *Since much of the Quarter's cast iron was added to previously-existing buildings, the Gauche house is unusual in having been designed with it from the beginning. The house is a simple rectangular volume with a service ell around the rear courtyard. Against its plain stucco walls and simple window frames the cast iron patterns stand out, in somewhat the same way wrought iron arabesques showed up against Spanish Colonial buildings. Details from the house illustrate several patterns of cast iron used in different ways. The palette of ironwork is varied but limited by the designer's desire for coherence.*

CL22 *The balcony railing is a repetition of rectangles in which the figure of a boy is inscribed within a frame of plant forms. A roof edged with ironwork above and below projects over the balcony, and pairs of iron brackets help support it.*

RKm22 *Granite frames the cast iron gates. The horizontal lines of the fence continue across the gates, maintaining a fairly tight discipline on patterns which, if used in too much profusion, would become confusing.*

RKm19A *The balcony and its roof nearly surround the building, seen here from the courtyard. Patterns of the ironwork are printed in shadow on the building's wall planes. Shadows change in size, shape and location as the sun moves.*

CL22 Gauche house

CL22 detail of balcony railing

CL22 *Surrounded by grape vines and carrying a wreath or a tambourine, a bacchant parades around the balcony like one repeating frame in a film of Carnival.*

RKm22 Gauche house, 704 Esplanade Avenue, 1856

RKm19A Gauche house

LL26A Gauche house

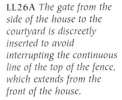

LL26A *The gate from the side of the house to the courtyard is discreetly inserted to avoid interrupting the continuous line of the top of the fence, which extends from the front of the house.*

RT6 1133 Chartres Street

CARRIAGEWAYS

A carriageways is a tunnel. When burrowed through the ground floor of the Creole town house, it allows a controlled current of people and sometimes breezes from street to courtyard. The term carriageway refers to the wider examples which could accommodate a vehicle. The French term *porte-cochère* is also used. Narrower versions, sometimes less than three feet, accommodate only people but work in the same way. The French called these *passages*, sometimes *corridors*. A carriageway is gated at the street, usually with wood, but generally ungated at the courtyard.

RT6 *Two carriageways extend each other across intervening Chartres Street. If the courtyard and figures in the foreground suggest Italy, this site is near St. Mary's Church, the focal point of a substantial Italian-American community in the late nineteenth and early twentieth centuries.*

RH723C *Successive arches mark the carriageway, the loggia and the courtyard of the Nicolas house. There are layered degrees of privacy. A wrought-iron gate secures the inner residential zones of the house from the street. Commercial space, on the other side of the wall to the right, opens to the street directly.*

RH723C Nicolas house, 723 Toulouse Street

MW 172 location unidentified, possibly 837 Royal Street

MW91 location unidentified, possibly the courtyard of the building in the photograph above

MW100 location unidentified

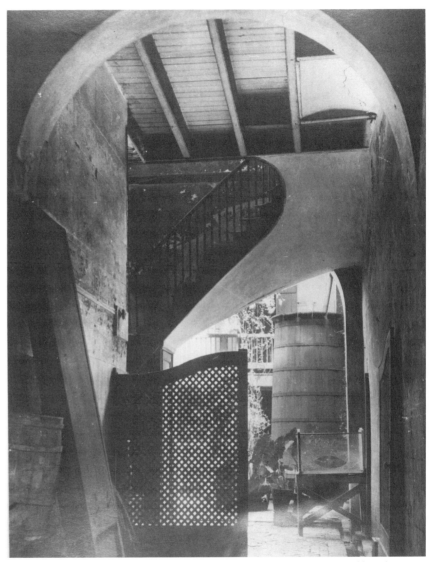

M15 400 block of Royal Street, possibly in a building demolished for the Civil Courts Building of 1907

MW172, MW91, MW100
Three Morgan Whitney photographs show views of carriageways—one from the street, one from a spare courtyard and one from the dark space of the carriageway itself. The reflective line at the right side of the bottom photograph may represent drainage to the street.

M15 *The surge of the stair at the end of this carriageway is a little unexpected. More typically it would be located at the opposite end of the loggia, out of view from the street. Cisterns like the one in this courtyard collected rainwater from the roofs for household use.*

101

K88 825 Bienville Street

K88 An arrangement of fixed louvers filters light and air on the upper level of this loggia. The lower level is open, connecting to and enlarging the courtyard space

RA42 The diagram reveals the loggia as a three-dimensional screen across the rear of the Creole town house. As circulation for the residential upper portion of the house, it connects directly with the carriageway and the street.

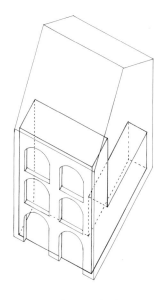

RA42 axonometric diagram of a three-story loggia

LOGGIAS

The open space of the carriageway generally flows into a loggia, a covered zone usually extending the depth of the courtyard and opening to it through a series of arches. The loggia is not an appendage—it is within of the volume of the building and occurs at each floor. In the typical Creole townhouse it contains the principal stairway for the building, leading to upper level loggias. These upper spaces are commonly arched and enclosed with glass, the fan-shaped transoms often photographed. Upper level loggias, glazed but quite open at their stairwells, provide one of the subtle "in-between" degrees of enclosure which characterize French Quarter buildings. The principal rooms of the house open to the courtyard through the loggia. The spatial transition from enclosed space, to covered but more open space, to the uncovered courtyard provides the sequence of shade to light so seductive when glimpsed through an open gate or from an interior room.

M22 unidentified town house, probably on Royal Street

RT14 628-30 Toulouse Street

MW174 unidentified, probably the Bosque house, 617-19 Chartres Street

M22 *A characteristic loggia for a larger town house has three levels of arches beside an extended service ell. The resulting courtyard is relatively long, narrow, and shady.*

RT14 *A stairway rises behind the arch to an upper level of the loggia. Stone paving is arranged to provide drainage for rain. It may have served the makeshift lavatory as well.*

MW174 *A wide arch and a narrow arch are repeated in shorter versions at the second level where their shapes are filled with casements and fanlights.*

K32 617 Dumaine Street

CL30 908 Esplanade Avenue

CL30, K32, K220, RKm19B *Courtyards are rooms and are given distinct character by the tastes of their owners. Originally most of them were places where laundry hung to dry or chickens scampered. But in the twentieth century those uses have given way to gardening and lounging. The earlier appearance of severity, order, and utility have been replaced by an ideal of lushness. The large, sheltering leaves of banana trees have been especially favored. They grow tall in a single season.*

COURTYARDS

French Quarter houses commonly extend to the edges of their property lines, with the house's inner walls held back about a court-yard. Courtyards vary widely in size and shape, with unpredictable lengths and widths. The heights of their enclosing walls can be wildly different, as they may belong to much larger or smaller adjacent buildings.

The courtyard and the French Quarter townhouse have the same relationship as the shifting images used by Gestalt psychologists—either the closed space of the house or the open space of the courtyard can be read

K220 615 Ursulines Street

RKm19B Gauche house, 704 Esplanade Avenue

as "figure" or "ground." The importance of this interdependence is the integral quality of the courtyard to this house type; neither part works or makes sense without the other. Nor is the garden of the Garden District house (or any other suburban arrangement) integral in the same way. The courtyard and the townhouse, because they exist within such tight limits of space, actually *shape* each other; one is the precise limit of its complement.

Light and air enter most rooms of the town house through the courtyard; without it the rooms would be dark and still. Courtyard walls are sometimes solid planes of brick or stucco. More often they are composed with several levels of the house's windows, doors, shutters, balconies, railings and perhaps stairs. Courtyards are a great place to study architectural scale because so many parts from different buildings come together in the middles of blocks. Unlike façades, which tend to be planar, courtyards provide juxtapositions of volume—the slender shed-roofed prism of a service structure, the horizontal void of a loggia, the tall gable-ended mass of an adjacent town house.

RA43 courtyard figure/ground

RK37 1013-15 Chartres Street

RK37 *The observatory-like protrusion on the rear of this brick town house contains a stair. Not a normal part of the French Quarter lexicon of shapes, this cylinder appears encumbered by the makeshift arrangement of porches and courtyard clutter around it. Today's situation is even less sympathetic. It sits with a new staircase but little spirit near the swimming pool of a motor hotel.*

The space of a courtyard may be quite tight, seen from an aerial photograph. A common shape is a long, narrow rectangular solid lying between its own equally narrow service structure and the adjacent property. But the aerial view describes only what is roofed and what is not; it does not show the in-between spaces under the roof that perceptually enlarge the courtyard when one inhabits it. Standing on the ground one looks into the open ground floor of the loggia or up into the balcony/corridors edging a service structure. The *perceived* space flows into these volumes, and even into an open pair of casement doors.

And again, spaces that look impossibly small or awkward in a plan drawing can be actually compelling because New Orleans light is so intense that a little of it is sufficient to enliven them. A banana tree will send up its broken leaf tops to be painted by the sun, and those flashing ribbons satisfy the eye, while the body is thankful for the cooler damp shade below.

Today visits to courtyards are conducted like garden tours in old suburbs. Courtyards are ornamented with fountains, pools, and prized flora and are thought of as places of leisure. This would not have been the case when they were built. Essentially utilitarian, courtyards accommodated among the subtropical plants such back-yard activities as drying laundry and raising livestock. Larger establishments had their own stables. In such a setting the scents of jasmine and orange blossoms would have masked less pleasant smells, and fig trees or the "crisp boughs of the pomegranate" described by George Washington Cable yielded fruit for the table.

K106 612-18 Bourbon Street

MW102 location unidentified

K106, MW102 *Behind solid street walls, the centers of French Quarter blocks are relatively open. Pieces of separately-owned houses juxtapose in compositions of angled roofs, brick walls, and wood fences. Windows at many levels give separate frames to these compositions from inside the buildings. Outside, the windows themselves are compositional elements.*

CL28 *As late as 1940, when Clarence Laughlin took this photograph, there was at least one courtyard in the Quarter where sheep lived. Rainwater from the roof of the two-story service building supplied the cistern through the downspout at right.*

CL28 831 Gov. Nicholls Street

MW77 *The soft light of Morgan Whitney's photograph harmonizes a hodgepodge of pipes, supports, and angled building pieces. There is a bridge overhead, probably a connection from the main building to a service structure.*

MW77 unidentified courtyard

Lafcadio Hearn penned the following description of the courtyard of a Creole household. Modern research says the twentieth century has romanticized the courtyard which was actually a place for lowly work and service activities. Writing as far back as 1879 Hearn described a decidedly civilized place, with no mention of work, let alone poultry. But then Hearn was a romantic.

Like many of the Creole houses, the façade presented a commonplace and unattractive aspect. The great green doors of the arched entrance were closed; and the green shutters of the balconied windows were half shut, like sleepy eyes lazily gazing upon the busy street below or the cottony patches of light clouds which floated slowly, slowly across the deep blue of the sky above. But beyond the gates lay a little Paradise. The great court, deep and broad, was framed in tropical green; vines embraced the white pillars of the piazza, and creeping plants climbed up the

MW78 unidentified courtyard

MW96 unidentified courtyard

MW98 unidentified courtyard

MW78, MW96, MW98
French Quarter courtyards are often taller than wide. Light, quite bright on upper walls, softens by the time it reaches the ground. Such furnishings as plants and lattice screens multiply shadow, giving a look of coolness. Floors are paved and plants may sit about in pots, moved from season to season to follow or avoid the sun. Traditional paving materials are local brick or imported bluestone.

tinted walls to peer into the upper windows with their flower-eyes of flaming scarlet. Banana-trees nodded sleepily their plumes of emerald green at the farther end of the garden; vines smothered the windows of the dining-room, and formed a bower of cool green about the hospitable door; an aged fig-tree, whose gnarled arms trembled under the weight of honeyed fruit, shadowed the square of bright lawn which formed a natural carpet in the midst; and at intervals were stationed along the walks in large porcelain vases— like barbaric sentinels in sentry-boxes—gorgeous broad-leaved things, with leaves fantastic and barbed and flowers brilliant as hummingbirds. A fountain murmured faintly near the entrance of the western piazza; and there came from the shadows of the fig-tree the sweet and plaintive cooing of amorous doves. Without, cotton-floats might rumble, and street-cars vulgarly jingle their bells; but these were mere echoes of the harsh outer world which disturbed not the delicious quiet within...

Lafcadio Hearn
"A Creole Courtyard"
Creole Sketches, 1879.[6]

CL26 Gaillard cottage, 917 St. Ann Street

RK1 641 Barracks Street, seen from Royal

CL26 A pair of tiny two-story service structures, each with a chimney and a balcony, are symmetrically placed behind a Creole cottage.

RK1 An L-shaped balcony connects this service structure with its main building.

RH820A Larger houses have larger service buildings. That of the Hermann-Grima house is three-stories tall and completely detached from the main building. Each upper room opens to a balcony which serves in lieu of any interior hallway.

RH820A Hermann-Grima House, 820 St. Louis Street

SERVICE BUILDINGS AND WINGS

On the Quarter's long, narrow lots service activities moved logically to the rear. Service structures opened to the courtyard and were related to the main house by varying degrees of connection. Often they were completely detached, forming a separate structure across the rear of the property. Other times they formed an ell with the main house. And sometimes both these approaches combined into an ell with an ell—an L-shaped structure set behind the main building.

Service structures had several functions and are known by several names. Old plans may use the term *cuisine* (kitchen)—they normally contained rooms used for cooking and food preparation. Actual cooking spaces are identifiable by a larger-than-usual fireplace. Slave quarter refers to the fact that house slaves would have had rooms in them before emancipation. Free servants used the same spaces

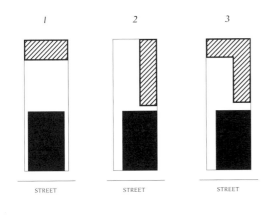

RA44 siting diagrams for service structures

■■■ MAIN BUILDING ///// SERVICE STRUCTURE

K221 722-24 Ursulines Street, c. 1829

RA44 *Service structures could be located (1)across the rear of a lot, (2)as an ell to the main building, or (3)as an ell with an ell of its own.*

K221 *The principal structure on this site is missing, and this service building now sits with a spacious garden between it and the street. Behind, it has an ell of its own which was used as a stable in the nineteenth century.*

after the War. A third term is *garçonnière*, referring to the custom of placing the bedrooms of boys of the household outside the main house once they reached a certain age. Service buildings were also places for household work or for the support of trades particular to specific dwellers. Today they are most often apartments. They may also be guest suites or studios or may serve a host of other uses. Occasionally they are still kitchens, separated from the main body of the house and renovated to include an informal eating area.

Ceiling heights are generally lower in the service buildings, and rooms are smaller. Hence these structures make up a somewhat different order or sub-type of building, becoming, for our purposes, another component available to the French Quarter builder. Narrow balconies provide the principal circulation for these buildings, connecting to the ground with

K5 629 Burgundy Street

K5 *The single-slope profile of this roof is a clear indication of a service structure. The narrow width, brick parapet, and wooden porch are other common features. This one stands free, but others may be attached to a main structure.*

111

K64, RKm6 *Photographed similarly, these two service ells differ in scale and detail. The Royal Street structure sits behind a Creole cottage. The other service wing is attached to a carefully-detailed five-bay Creole town house. In addition to being half again as long, the Tricou structure has turned posts rather than the simpler box posts of the other. The full floor height of the Tricou house is carried through to the rear wing, making it unusually grand scaled. Openings in both structures are a combination of casement doors and double-hung windows.*

K64 1021 Royal Street

RKm6 Tricou house, 709-713 Bourbon Street

K165 *The upper window here indicates a half story. It is somewhat unusual to find a service building less than a full two stories. Its profile resembles the side of a Creole cottage cut in half.*

K165 831 Gov. Nicholls Street

stairways, often open ones set within the body of the service structure. In cases where balconies connect to the main house, adjustments had to be made to account for variations in ceiling heights; the insertion of short runs of stairs in the balconies are the surprising and often graceful result.

The roofs of service structures have one-directional slopes, draining water into the courtyard or into cisterns before city water was available. This shed-roof shape, often with angled brick parapets at the ends and balconies along one side, is a highly recognizable French Quarter building block.

K10 1120 Burgundy Street

K115 827 Bourbon Street

K4 531-33 Burgundy Street

K10 *When modern plumbing came along it was attached to French Quarter structures in straightforward ways. Adding plumbing, in this case, didn't necessarily mean indoor plumbing.*

K4 *Two or three stories is the usual height for service buildings. A wooden balcony structure may project, as here, from inside the brick end walls. The brick walls continue up and terminate in a parapet.*

K115 *Service buildings normally require stairs separate from those of the main structure. Placing stairs within an open arch is a common solution.*

RH1301 *The rear of these town houses is visible across an open lot on Barracks Street. Three-story service structures are attached to three-story town houses. Some of the structures are partly or mostly missing, but pieces of the single-slope roof shape carry on the original rhythm. Courtyard spaces between the buildings would be characteristically long, narrow and tall.*

RH1301 rear view of town house row facing the 1200 block of Decatur Street

K129 *An L-shaped service structure appears over a courtyard wall. The ell attaches to the main part of the house, a corner structure.*

K129 701 Burgundy Street

The familiar shed-roofed profile of a service building, the end of a prism with galleries attached, often shows up on streets. The end of a service structure can acknowledge its street position by becoming a kind of front, with a door to the street. Perhaps a gallery on the courtyard side of the structure will extend around the building's corner and shelter a piece of the street. In this way the buildings develop a public side, and many of them in the upper Quarter are used as shops today. Other times a row of service buildings becomes visible from the street across some open space, setting up a rhythm of repetitive shapes. These shapes compose and juxtapose with other familiar building shapes. All these shapes become the "words" in an identifiable urban language that is at once both varied and coherent.

M20 633 Toulouse Street

K2 841 Bourbon Street, seen from Dumaine

M20 *The three-story service structure has a gallery that extends from the courtyard onto the street. Originally two stories, it was built to serve the corner building in the foreground. With its added third floor it has a strong street presence in its own right.*

K2 *The tall and narrow shape of this three-story service structure abuts the street. Placement of house, courtyard and service structure on a narrow lot can be seen as a negotiation for space. Making the buildings taller allows more space for the courtyard.*

K81 707 Barracks Street

RK107 1012 St. Philip Street

K81 *Seeing this hip-roofed service structure from the street, one thinks of it as an independent building. It can even be imagined as a miniature version of the typical Charleston house, its side gallery overlooking a narrow courtyard instead of a garden.*

RK107 *Both a door and a window from this service structure open to the street. Its width is nearly that of a two-bay Creole cottage. But its narrow street front and considerable depth bring to mind a two-story shotgun.*

RK86D 817-19 St. Ann Street

RK86D *This combination of options—the split-level* cabinet *within the one-and-three-quarter cottage—begins to suggest the richness of choice possible when variants of a limited number of types* and *components of buildings are combined. The glazed gallery archway is one of a pair.*

K141 *Makeshift exterior stairs lead to the upper level of this house, or perhaps just to the upper level of a cabinet. Normally any such stairs would be inside.*

K141 address uncertain

THE CABINET/GALLERY ASSEMBLY

This component is a linear arrangement of three spaces—two small closed *cabinets* at either end and a larger gallery, open or with glazed doors, in the center. The *cabinets* (usually pronounced in French, cah-bee-nay) were generally used as service rooms or children's bedrooms. One might contain a stairway. *Cabinets* open to the gallery and only sometimes to the larger rooms adjacent to them. Sometimes a *cabinet* is divided by a floor, forming a low, cellar-like space below (known as a *cave*) and usable space above. The gallery opens generously to the outdoors. When the gallery openings are glazed they normally have wide and full-length casement doors; they suggest an outdoor space only momentarily enclosed. As a spatial idea the *cabinet*/gallery sequence is wonderfully effective; by inserting a central gallery into a building's rear range of rooms, all the adjacent rooms obtain access to its light and air and, by extension, to the courtyard behind it.

The *cabinet*/gallery assembly happens at many scales, from modest to grand. It is standard on most Creole cottages, but it also occurs at Madame John's Legacy, at the Beauregard House (see p. 46) and in a stacked, two-story version at the Hermann-Grima House. Jay Edwards notes its early use in New Orleans and its even earlier use on Hispaniola, and suggests European origins.[7] Outside New Orleans it is found in local plantation houses as well as in town houses in Natchez and elsewhere. The symmetrical arrangement of a wide space flanked by narrower ones also brings to mind the standard New England five-room plan in which a relatively wide kitchen sits at the rear of a house between two smaller rooms. There, adjacency to a central chimney is more important than access to a rear yard. Though striking, the formal similarity is doubtless an accident.

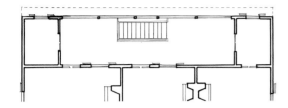

Madame John's Legacy, detail of plan on page 18

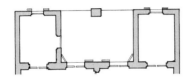

La Rionda house, detail of plan on page 28

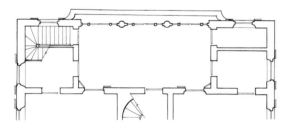

Hermann-Grima House, detail of plan on page 47

RK105C 931-33 St. Philip Street

RH820B Hermann-Grima House, 820 St. Louis Street

Plans, RH820B *The cabinet/ gallery sequence occurs at various scales, at various times, and on various building types. The long gallery at Madame John's Legacy dates from 1788. It may copy an earlier French Colonial plan. The arrangement at the La Rionda cottage is standard for Creole cottages, this one dating from around 1810. At the Hermann-Grima House the cabinets and gallery appear at the rear of a center- hall American town house. They repeat at the upper level.*

RK105C, RK105D *The upper cabinet opening on this 1805 cottage works something like a window on a stair landing. With its doors tightly shut in the lower photograph, it suggests the English use of the term cabinet, looking too small for anything but an enclosed storage container with two unlikely steps peeping out.*

RK105D 931-33 St. Philip Street

GLOSSARY OF STYLES

THE MATTER OF STYLE

Style is something every builder and architect thinks about. Builders' attention to style has given us some of the most delightful moments in French Quarter buildings. But assessing the importance of style is tricky business, since its importance varies enormously from building to building.

This book contends that French Quarter buildings are more likely to be distinguished by their development of type than of style. That is, the real innovations they represent, the new syntheses they forge from the nature of their place and the forces of their inherited cultures, occur in the modifications and developments of type rather than in the development and refinement of style. Architectural styles arrived by ship to this port city, rather like fashions in clothing, to be successively draped on the same persisting and evolving typological bodies. It is the evolution of these typological bodies which sets the Quarter's buildings apart. Type responds both to New Orleans' cultural circumstances *and* to its peculiar geography. Its accommodation to heat and the constant presence of water—in the River, in the ground, in the air—set it apart from other American cities.

Style, on the other hand, is almost purely cultural—a recognizable manner of attending to the making of buildings as transmitted within a given culture. In the French Colonial and Spanish Colonial periods of New Orleans, such cultural imprint was clear and direct—the Ursuline Convent was built by a French engineer who knew French models, and it looks like buildings in France and other French colonies of the same period, c. 1750. The French colonial builders' addition of galleries to these structures in the manner of West Indian houses was an alteration to the type more than a change of style. Spanish Colonial structures in New Orleans (1763-1803) similarly reflect Spanish models of style and models from other Spanish colonies, though they have the additional complexity of having been overlaid on an existing French Colonial and African-American population with its own stylistic predilections and a continuing craft tradition.

Things became no simpler as Anglo-American builders arrived in numbers after the Louisiana Purchase. A preponderance of French builders remained, at least for a while. New Anglo-American styles were not adopted wholesale, but were rather assimilated into the existing building practices, along with contemporary influences from France and the West Indies. (Thousands of refugees from the slave uprisings on the island of Hispaniola arrived during the same general period of time as the Louisiana Purchase.) So French and

RT5 The Cabildo's façade of the 1790s shows the fan windows, wrought ironwork and classical columns which also appeared on the larger residences in the Spanish Colonial style. This Frances Benjamin Johnston photograph communicates the style's characteristic weight.

Spanish and African stylistic impulses—they have come gradually to be combined in the term Creole—survived alongside the full range of nineteenth-century styles, which themselves intermingled.

For perspective we return to the often-noted oddity that New Orleans has always existed as an island, physically and culturally remote from any mainstream, yet cosmopolitan enough to be in touch with several. Sorting through strands of architectural style in all this is a bit like analyzing the city's cuisine—one always ends up with a gumbo analogy. Beyond that, one needs a recipe or at least a list of

ingredients for this stylistic gumbo, which is what this section of the book provides. More accurately it presents a sort of reverse recipe, an analysis. One tastes the buildings and figures out the ingredients.

Hence the use of a *glossary*—a compendium of styles which have affected French Quarter buildings, together with graphic illustrations of their effect. Because style leaves its mark on all types of buildings, the examples used in this section need not be limited to the types previously discussed; ecclesiastical and public buildings are pictured as well as residential structures.

K175C, photo c. 1946

K175A, C *A pair of photographs, taken within a year of each other, shows the remodeling of an Italianate façade at 819 Orleans (K175A) into a simpler version of itself (K175C). The wood siding, the quoins and the enframements around the openings were replaced with stucco; the front door was given a flat Greek Revival frame; and the decorated gable was removed from the roof. Whether these changes came of pure preference or of some necessity such as a fire, they show an intention to have a simpler, "earlier" style, presumably considered more tasteful.*

K175A 819 Orleans Street, c. 1890, photographed c. 1945

FRENCH COLONIAL

DATES: PERIOD OF FRENCH RULE: 1718-1763. FRENCH ARCHITECTURE AND PLANNING TRADITIONS ESTABLISHED THE BASIC SHAPE OF THE COLONIAL TOWN, AND THE RESULTING STYLISTIC CHARACTER EXTENDED FAR AFTER 1763, STILL SHOWING UP, FOR EXAMPLE, IN STEEPLY HIPPED-ROOF COTTAGES BUILT LATE IN THE SPANISH COLONIAL PERIOD, THE 1780S AND 90S.

Stylistic elements of French Colonial buildings track the architecture of simple buildings in France and Canada of the time. Roofs are steep and hipped, with especially steep pitches at the ends of structures. Windows and doors are casements, with relatively small panes and often segmentally-arched tops. Dormers were small when they occurred. Cross-timbering was occasionally exposed for visual effect, but this was quickly found impractical in the New Orleans climate, and surfaces were covered with stucco or wide, beaded weatherboards. Consonant with the colder climates from which the architectural tradition came, the earliest buildings did not have galleries to protect their walls from the sun or their windows from rain. But by 1750 galleries were being designed for New Orleans buildings and roofs assumed a double slope.

LL17 Ursuline Convent, 1100 Chartres Street, 1745-50 (entrance portico c. 1890)

MH61 Lafitte's Blacksmith Shop, 939-41 Bourbon Street, probably after 1781

MH8 Ursuline Convent, detail of roof profile

RT8 Madame John's Legacy, 628-32 Dumaine Street, 1788

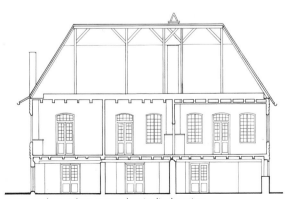

RA45 Madame John's Legacy, longitudinal section

LL17 The Ursuline Convent is the only building known to survive relatively intact from the French Colonial period.

MH61, MH8 The steep end roof with a gentle curve at the end, characteristic of the French Colonial style, also appears on the Bourbon Street cottage, built well into the Spanish Colonial period.

RT8, RA45 Madame John's steep French Colonial roof is double-pitched in the short direction to shelter a gallery.

121

SPANISH COLONIAL

DATES: PERIOD OF SPANISH RULE, 1763-1803. SPANISH ARCHITECTURAL INFLUENCE WAS NOT FELT IMMEDIATELY IN DETERMINEDLY GALLIC NEW ORLEANS. BUT ONCE ESTABLISHED, ELEMENTS OF SPANISH COLONIAL MASSING AND DETAILING PERSISTED WELL INTO THE NINETEENTH CENTURY.

Although most builders working in the city were still French in the 1780s and 90s, a more weighty and horizontal Spanish esthetic prevailed on the important buildings—wide two-story structures with florid ironwork set off against expanses of massive stuccoed walls, sometimes punctuated with classical pilasters. Round-headed and elliptical arches were used in combination with square-topped openings in expanses of stuccoed masonry walls. Roofs with shallow slopes, sometimes almost flat, replaced the steep French roofs, strengthening an effect of horizontality. There were casement windows and doors and fanlight transoms. Wood trim sometimes included carved rafter ends. On façades, flat bands of raised plaster often surrounded doors and windows and marked the edges of walls. The walls of more elaborate structures had pilaster-like arrangements of quoins and heavy molded cornices. The shallow roofs sometimes had balustrades made of open tile work or wrought iron panels between pedestals. This is the finest period for the French Quarter's hand-wrought iron railings, the iron attenuated into spiraling curves, circles and ovals.

RT2 Cabildo, Jackson Square, 1795-99, Gilberto Guillemard, architect, Marcellino Hernandez, ironworker

RT2, LL1, MW136, RH533
The Cabildo, if imagined without its 1847 mansard roof addition, is solid and horizontal with stout corners and classical detailing. Spanish Colonial houses have the same horizontal street presence, their openings and corners marked by plaster banding.

ARH10 *The design of the wrought iron railing at the Presbytère compresses strong energy and movement within a tightly restricted frame. The identity of the iron worker is uncertain.*

ARH10 wrought iron panel from the Presbytère, Jackson Square

LL1 Rillieux house, 337-43 Royal Street, c. 1800, attributed to Barthélemy Lafon

MW164 Orue-Pontalba house (shown long before its 1962 reconstruction as part of Le Petit Théâtre) 1796, Gilberto Guillemard, architect, Hilaire Boutté, builder, Marcellino Hernandez, iron worker

MW164 *The Orue-Pontalba house was built across St. Peter Street from the Cabildo by the same architect and builder with railings by the same gifted iron worker.*

RH723B *New Orleans builders of Spanish Colonial times favored beam ends carved into fluid shapes. Such stylistic preferences continued beyond the strict dates of Spanish political control.*

MW136 Montegut house, 729-733 Royal Street, c. 1795

RH533 Napoleon House, two-story portion at 535-37 St. Louis Street, 1798

RH723B 723 Toulouse,1808, Hilaire Boutté. builder

123

MW1 Louisiana State Bank building, 401-03 Royal Street, designed 1820, completed 1822, Benjamin Henry Latrobe, architect; Benjamin Fox, builder

FEDERAL
DATES: C. 1800-1840

A gradual lightening of components and details began in French Quarter buildings around the turn of the nineteenth century. Federal details enhanced, in particular, the large number of Creole town houses which, by the 1820s and 30s, were becoming numerous and relatively uniform in plan. They became some of the Quarter's most elegant buildings. Their street-front simplicity was a foil for transoms with thin, thin muntins and refined wrought iron work in simple geometrical patterns. Graceful dormers had double-hung sashes with arched or segmental heads and patterns of curving muntins. Carved wooden cornices with swag designs became common at roof lines.

MW1, RA46 *Benjamin Henry Latrobe, architect of the U.S. Capitol and pre-eminent with his friend Thomas Jefferson in American architecture in his day, designed this building just before he died in New Orleans of yellow fever. The circular hall and shallow vaulting of the main banking spaces are unique in New Orleans. They distantly recall the hovering saucer domes of English architect John Soane's Bank of England, work Latrobe would have known. Soane would have found a way to bring natural light to the dome, a possibility precluded here by the bank cashier's apartment on the upper floor.*

K50 *Exterior forms are smooth and cubic, with balconies lightly attached. Because there are two roof structures within the building, it is assumed that the bank was built with a nearly-flat roof and no dormers. The newer roof, parapet, and dormers, however, were skillfully made.*

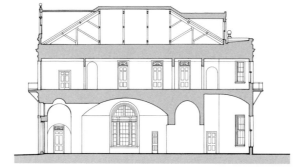

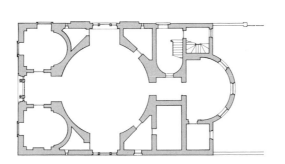

RA46 Louisiana State Bank, longitudinal section and ground floor plan

K50 Louisiana State Bank

RH536ChB Gally houses, , detail, 536 Chartres Street

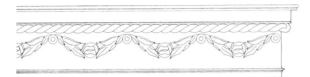

RA47 Gurlie and Guillot cornice

RK81B 624 Royal Street, 1831

RH536ChB, RA47, RK72
Gurlie and Guillot were a pair of skillful architect/builders who constructed many town houses in the Quarter. A wood cornice in a pattern of ropes and swags is almost a signature of their work. The detail of the Vignie houses shows other typical elements of town houses of the 1820s and 30s—box balconies with wrought iron railings, a carefully detailed transom, and lintels with a three-block design.

RK81B A carefully-made wooden cornice and subtly-detailed dormer were common on Federal town houses. Upper and lower parts of these shutters are hinged separately to allow the upper ones to open fully.

RK72 Vignie houses, 713-719 Royal Street, 710-14 Orleans Street, 1831, Gurlie and Guillot

K161 334-38 Exchange Place, c. 1835

K161 This arch and its neighbors are part of an arcaded row planned by J.N.B. DePouilly to run the length of Exchange Place. The plan is only partially realized. A series of arched openings was the usual treatment for the ground-floor façades of Federal-style buildings in the Quarter.

125

MW5 Bank of Louisiana building, 334-40 Royal Street, 1826, Bickle, Hamblet and Fox, builders

By whatever routes they may have come to New Orleans, the delicate linearity of the English Adam style was evident together with, in places, the simplifying geometries of French Neoclassicism. These stylistic impulses show up in details as well as in the shapes of rooms and in the overall massing of buildings. Occasionally Federal style buildings were designed with columned porticos, speaking architectural Latin by using one of the classical Roman orders. The Federal details and the classicism in these cases were lighter, softer and more curving than the coming Greek Revival was to offer. Red brick came into common use with, often, the material itself as well as the fashion imported from East Coast cities.

MW5 A temple form is suggested by the two-story Tuscan half-columns on the street faces of this bank structure. Such Federal style classicism was restrained, more Roman, and somewhat more delicate than that of the later Greek Revival.

MW9 The round arch of this door helps to identify this structure with the Federal style. The blocked window lintels are carved marble.

LL9 Granite blocks are shaped into voussoirs to form the ground-floor arches of this five-bay house. It is much more common in the Quarter to find granite used for square openings and for arches to be made of plastered brick.

MW9 Bank of Louisiana building, Conti Street entrance

LL9 Boimaré-McCarty house, 509-11 Royal Street, 1832

RT9 Old Absinthe House, 234-40 Bourbon Street, c. 1806

RT4 Hermann-Grima House, 812-20 St. Louis Street, 1831, William Brand

M28 Tricou house, 709-713 Bourbon Street, c.1832-34, Gurlie and Guillot

M18, Hermann-Grima House, front door

RT9 *The geometry of this building is clear and cubic. Its balconies are treated to appear light and not to distract from the massing. Similarly, there is no exterior expression of the entresol level, the windows of which occur in the semi-circles of the arches. Openings are minimal and carefully spaced.*

M28 *This Creole town house shows a generous five bay façade to the street. Its wider central arch accommodates a carriageway. Gurlie and Guillot gave it their trademark wooden cornice.*

RT4, M18 *The substantial free-standing mass of the Hermann-Grima House is a Federal-style anomaly in the French Quarter, where most town houses share common walls. Its gabled profile and its careful Federal doorways would be at home in more typically American cities of the period.*

MW129 Pontalba Buildings, Jackson Square, 1849-50, James Gallier, Sr., original architect; Henry Howard, architect of final plans

MW129 *The Pontalba Buildings have the flat granite lintels, as well as the posts, gables, and trim pieces commonly used on Greek Revival buildings in the French Quarter. Windows are double-hung with relatively large panes of glass and sashes large enough to give access to the galleries and balconies which surround the buildings.*

CL3 620 St. Peter Street, c. 1838, David Sidle and Samuel Stewart, builders

CL3 *The doorway of this tall town house is heavily decorated with Greek Revival motifs. The three horizontal windows within the cornice, fitted with panels of cast iron, give light to the attic level without complicating the massing as dormers would do.*

RKm1, K99 *The anthemion is a stylized floral form used in Greek Revival decoration. Two somewhat different radiating clusters, a tall one of cast iron and a semi-circular one of wood, appear on a gate and a door enframement.*

RKm1 gate, Jackson Square

GREEK REVIVAL
DATES: 1835-1860 AND BEYOND

The strength and simplicity of Greek Classicism attracted the admiration of French Quarter builders. They used Greek forms and syntax, and they reinterpreted them in particular local ways, as other builders did across the country and in Europe. While small urban lots allowed few free-standing temples or temple fronts, town houses could have columned porticos and such Greek Revival staples as boldly-scaled six over six windows, solid two- and four-paneled doors, and the so-called Greek key door and window surrounds. Arches became less popular (except in the work of the Frenchman de Pouilly). They were replaced by rectangular openings with flat lintels. Granite, imported from Northeastern quarries, became common as trim. Granite blocks were inset as lintels in red brick walls, and many ground-floor commercial frontages became a succession of hefty granite posts and lintels. Ceilings moved higher, and the scale of detail became weightier and more emphatic. Grander entranceways might include a pair of solid paneled doors protecting a small exterior vestibule with a second door beyond surrounded by sidelights and a transom. A carved anthemion crest might crown a door frame;

K99 414-16 Bourbon Street, c. 1840

MW10 U.S. Mint, 400 Esplanade Avenue, Willliam Strickland, 1835, Benjamin Fox and John Mitchell, builders

RK19 335 Chartres Street, c. 1830

MW10 *William Strickland's U.S. Mint presents a strong Ionic temple front to Esplanade Avenue. Columns are plastered brick, with granite bases and capitals. A symmetrical pair of granite stairways is concealed behind the wall at the base of the columns. The run of the stairs is parallel to the street.*

RK19 *Granite posts and lintels frame the street-level openings of this structure, one of a row of three. The repetition of such pillars is a rhythmic component of many blocks in the upper Quarter. These doors are known as night blinds. Their glazed panels can be covered by removable wooden panels at night.*

MW59 *James H. Dakin's use of the Greek Revival style favored boldly-scaled forms, strong and square, which are singularly appropriate to his imposing 1839 Arsenal.*

MW59 Arsenal, 615 St. Peter Street, 1839

129

K169, MW33 *St. Louis Cathedral does not look like an American Greek Revival structure. Architect DePouilly arrived in New Orleans from France in 1833, and his version of international classicism did not require abandoning arches. The Cathedral façade celebrates arches, in fact, squeezing them between several orders of pilasters and paired columns. A pediment breaks around a clock, with the main spire set above it and smaller ones on octagonal towers to the sides. If the arrangement is not cutting-edge architecture for its time, it nevertheless has the scale necessary to hold its place on Jackson Square. Set at the city's historic center, its image has become emblematic of the Roman Catholic Church in New Orleans.*

LL31A *A strongly-molded Corinthian capital gives a hint of the character of the domed interior of the Merchants' Exchange, now destroyed.*

K169 St. Louis Cathedral, Jackson Square, 1850, J.N.B. de Pouilly

lyres and anthemions might be repeated on a cast iron railing. Such ornament also appeared in elaborate interior plaster work in both public and private structures. Dormers lost some of their popularity in favor of horizontal windows set within thick entablature-like bands just under roof lines.

The arrival of new architects strengthened local expertise in the Greek Revival—J. N. B. de Pouilly came from France in 1833 and James Gallier, Sr., and James Dakin arrived from New York in 1835. Dakin had been a partner of Town and Davis, New York architects known for their Greek Revival work, and Gallier, while in New York, was in partnership with Minard Lafever, author of influential pattern books which showed Greek Revival styling. Henry Howard, of Irish birth like Gallier (whose name is a Gallicized version of Gallagher), was an especially accomplished pupil of James Dakin; he designed some of Louisiana's finest nineteenth-century structures.

MW33 St. Louis Cathedral

LL31A Merchants' Exchange (destroyed by fire in 1960), 100 block of Royal Street, 1835, Charles Dakin and James Gallier, Sr.

RK18B Marble Hall, U.S. Custom House, 423 Canal Street, 1848-1881, A.T. Wood and others

RT10 French Opera House (destroyed by fire in 1919), 541 Bourbon Street, 1859, James Gallier, Jr.

M30 Thierry house, 721 Gov. Nicholls Street, 1814, Arsène Lacarrière Latour and Henry Boneval Latrobe

K126A 1303 Bourbon Street, c. 1840

RK18B *New Orleans' grandest Greek Revival interior is the counting room of the U.S. Custom House. The skylit space is surrounded by fourteen marble Corinthian columns, each forty-one feet high.*

RT10 *The central bays of the French Opera House projected and the curb of Bourbon Street shifted to accommodate arriving patrons. Abruptly larger than its neighbors, the Opera House asserted its pre-eminence in the city's cultural and social life.*

M30, K126A *An early incidence of local interest in Greek forms, the simple Doric columns of the Thierry house contrast tellingly with the stiff American probity of the Bourbon Street structure.*

MH52 1236 N. Rampart Street, former monastery of St. Joseph and St. Teresa of the Order of Discalced Carmelite Nuns, 1891, James Freret, architect

> ## THE MULTIPLICATION OF STYLES
>
> *The Greek Revival was the last style fully to affect architecture in the French Quarter during its robust years, the years of growth and prosperity prior to the Civil War. Thereafter the Greek Revival persevered in many buildings, along with modifications suggested by other stylistic developments. It was as if the advent of mass production had weakened the potency of style itself, with variations made rather mechanically onto a set group of building types.*

MH10 Labranche buildings, Cabildo Alley, c. 1840

K3 1121-25 Bourbon Street, c. 1890

GOTHIC REVIVAL

DATES: 1840-1870s

The application of Gothic arches, details and steep roofs excited little interest in the French Quarter except for religious structures. In the rest of the city some examples, if they can be called that, came in by the back door of mass production, as a few of the multitude of cast iron patterns used in decorative ironwork. But even these were rarely used in the Quarter.

MH52 *Of this half-block complex of buildings the Chapel, with its steep roof and lancet windows, is the most forthright expression of the Gothic Revival style. Inside is simple wooden trusswork, stained dark.*

MH10 *This pointed arch makes a surprise appearance on several rear doors of the Labranche buildings. It is unclear whether the builder had the Gothic Revival style in mind, or simply wanted to make a narrow arch as tall as the adjacent round arches.*

K3 *The steep Gothic gable seems determined to unify the binary nature of this double shotgun.*

ITALIANATE

DATES: 1850-1890 AND BEYOND

The wholesale addition of cast iron ornament to French Quarter buildings after 1850 marked a transition from the restraint of Greek Revival to an architecture of more pieces. That impulse also found expression in the Italianate style, with its brackets placed under eaves, its multiple moldings, and its variably shaped openings, especially segmental arches, themselves sometimes outlined in cast iron. Italianate buildings in New Orleans coincided with an increase in the use of manufactured parts, including the wooden brackets, quoins and moldings common on shotgun cottages. A rhythm of square cast iron columns with folding doors between became usual for the street fronts of ground floor commercial spaces. In 1866 at the edge of the French Quarter (111 Exchange Place) the Bank of America erected a five-story cast iron Italianate façade for a rental property behind its Canal Street location.

LL34 521-23 Royal Street, c. 1859, Peter Ross, builder

K1 address uncertain

MH22 1100-10 Royal Street, c. 1884, Thomas Sully, architect

K132 1000-08 Burgundy Street, destroyed

LL34 *The entire street-level façade of this building is cast iron. There is a lively rhythm of alternating large and small arches and heavy brackets.*

K1 *Manufactured wooden quoins, nailed onto flat boards, commonly mark the corners of Italianate houses.*

MH22 *Thomas Sully, architect of uptown houses in the Queen Anne style, designed this Italianate commercial structure to open to the street like a bazaar. Unfortunately the ground floor is now used for parking.*

K132 *Quoins, segmentally-arched windows, and brackets identify this building with the Italiante style. Such corner buildings are found throughout the city.*

MH66 *The gigantic columns of granite from Quincy, Massachusetts, support an entablature with a massive cornice of cast iron.*

MH66 U.S. Custom House, 423 Canal Street, 1848-1881, A.T. Wood & others

EGYPTIAN REVIVAL

DATES: MID-1800s

There was little interest in exotic architectural styles in the French Quarter with one monumental exception—the quartet of giant granite columns repeated on each of the four façades of the U.S. Custom House at the Quarter's edge (423 Canal Street). The sinuous forms of their capitals, as well as a continuous band of plant shapes on the cast iron entablature just below the dentils, repeat such motifs as the lotus that were associated with Egyptian rather than Greek or Roman design.

MH28 1309 Dauphine Street, c. 1886

MH28, MH3 *Two American town houses in the lower Quarter follow the same stylistic pattern— segmentally-arched openings, a covered second-level balcony, and a dormer with three windows set into the mansard roof*

MH3 634 Esplanade Avenue, 1885, Middlemiss and Murray, builders

SECOND EMPIRE

DATES: 1880s IN THE QUARTER; OFTEN EARLIER ELSEWHERE

Mansard roofs, usually with dormers, are the distinguishing characteristic of the Second Empire style, which was loosely inspired by the wings of the new Louvre built in Paris in the 1850s. They appear occasionally on New Orleans houses, including several in the lower Quarter. (The mansard roofs added to the Cabildo and the Presbytère in 1847 pre-date the popularization of this style. They, too, are probably the result of Parisian interests—the Baroness Pontalba proposed a scheme believed to have included them [since lost] to the city in 1846.[1] It is a curiosity that architect L.T.J. Visconti who is associated with the design of the mansarded pavilions of the new parts of the Louvre also designed the Baroness's house in Paris.[2])

QUEEN ANNE

DATES: C. 1900 IN THE QUARTER (OFTEN EARLIER ELSEWHERE)

Characterized by steep roofs, asymmetric massing and an active wall plane, the Queen Anne umbrella covers a wide range of buildings, loosely inspired by late medieval English and French precedents. There are a few conscious examples in the Quarter. More commonly Queen Anne is one of many styles overlaid on the shotgun type, the modest forms of which comprised the principal residential building activity in the Quarter at this time of its economic decline.

MH1 929-31 St. Louis Street, c. 1900

MH21 929-31 St. Louis Street

MH1, MH21 *This house is a Queen Anne style essay in the Creole cottage form. There is a narrow, two-story service ell behind.*

K159 *The corner tower of this commercial/residential structure appears to be lacking a complete roof form. Today it is even more truncated.*

K159 836-42 Esplanade Avenue, c. 1900

BEAUX ARTS

DATES: EARLY 1900s IN THE FRENCH QUARTER

In spite of the high-sounding name of this style, some of its French Quarter examples have been considered brash, out-of-scale and inappropriate, especially the Civil Courts Building at 400 Royal Street. The passage of time, however, has softened those evaluations. Other French Quarter examples show façades of restraint and refinement. Buildings in this style present an elaborate, studied classicism with an abundance of ornament. The bases of these buildings are (or simulate) rusticated stone.

B2 Historic New Orleans Collection Research Center, 410-14 Chartres Street, 1915, E.A. Christy, architect; J.A. Petty, contractor

MH26 Monteleone Hotel, 208-220 Royal Street, 1908, Toledano and Wogan

MH26 *The florid decorations of the Monteleone Hotel are executed in glazed terra cotta.*

B2 *The correct Beaux-Arts classicism of this former court building and police station must have contrasted sharply with its simpler neighbors, which were probably run down at the time it was built. Architect Christy was accomplished in a variety of styles; see pp. 136 and 138.*

135

MH24 1310 Royal Street, c.1925-30

MH24, K79 *The tapered square columns, plain wooden brackets and multi-paned casements of the Craftsman style affected the façades of these two variants of the shotgun house.*

K79 627-29 Barracks Street, c. 1910

CRAFTSMAN

DATES: EARLY DECADES OF THE 1900s

Popular for modest houses, the Craftsman style affected the façades of shotguns and doubles, mainly in the lower Quarter. The style is a distant American cousin of the English Arts and Crafts Movement, emphasizing the appearance, at least, of craft with exposed rafters and other wood structural members (often false). Roof pitches are low, overhangs wide. The typical Craftsman column is square with sloping sides; it is made of wood and often sits on a masonry pedestal.

MH29 Central Fire Station, 317 Decatur Street, 1913, E.A. Christy, architect, John Minot, contractor

MH29 *Here Christy's mode was a careful commercial/ public style. Spots of blue and green glazed terra cotta brighten the façade.*

MH20 215-225 Decatur Street, c. 1908, Emile Weil

EARLY TWENTIETH CENTURY INDUSTRIAL AND COMMERCIAL

DATES: FIRST DECADES OF THE 1900s

The construction of industrial-style buildings in the Quarter illustrates its decline as a residential district. The decline began after the Civil War and continued until the Preservation Movement in the 1920s and 30s. These plain-spoken buildings often have steel or concrete structural frames, allowing them wider spans and a distinctly horizontal arrangement of windows. They are larger than their neighbors, and their original uses were sometimes incompatible with a residential neighborhood. Today many have become residential and commercial establishments. Several, designed by architects skillful in a number of styles, achieve an admirable level of quality.

MH20 *Architect Weil, knowledgeable of classical composition, stylized the details of this glazed brick structure which he designed for a shoe company. Large industrial-scaled windows are set withing well-proportioned openings.*

SPANISH REVIVAL

DATES: 1920s-30s

Not surprisingly, this twentieth-century style has a pictorial kinship with the plaster walls and tile roofs of eighteenth-century Spanish Colonial buildings. Its dates coincide with the beginning of preservation activities in the Quarter. There are few full-fledged examples of the style, but intriguing snippets show up in renovations and new construction of that era. The temptation to be both historic and fashionable with the same style must have been too much to resist.

K20 Bosque house, 617-19 Chartres Street, 1795, stairway is twentieth century, detail

MH25, K20 *A Spanish mission inspired the design this church. The stairs added to the courtyard of the eighteenth-century Bosque house show a Spanish Revival style and spirit.*

MH25 St. Mark's United Methodist Church, 1126-40 N. Rampart Street, c. 1923

DEFINING TWENTIETH CENTURY PRESERVATIONIST STYLES

A strong impulse has been present since around 1920 to "preserve" the French Quarter. The movement that sprang from that impulse deserves enormous credit for the survival of the Quarter's remarkable inventory of buildings. Innovative legislation, especially the work of Jacob Morrison, constructed a legal framework for this movement in the 1930s, establishing the Vieux Carré Commission to oversee and restrict changes.[3] Almost by definition, "preservation" implies a defensive posture against forces of change and destruction. But the preservation impulse has also resulted in new ways of doing new building activities. Inevitably questions of style emerge here—what does one do with buildings that have changed over time? does one preserve the changes? to what degree does one "restore" and to what degree does one "renovate"? what style is appropriate for new construction within the architectural context of such a district? These have become some of the most interesting (and knotty) questions of

twentieth-century architecture, taking their place as major issues not only within official historic districts, but far beyond. Architectural thought was dominated by Modernism for half this century. The problem of bringing Modernism into some kind of rapprochement, or at least detente (the use of the language of diplomacy seems appropriate) with the urban matrix around it, and with the history of which it finds itself a chapter, has preoccupied thoughtful architects in recent decades.

The twentieth century, like the nineteenth, has had many architectural idioms. The Preservationist idiom can only be seen as one of them, existing alongside and often in conflict with Modernism. In the French Quarter, two identifiable styles have emerged within the constraints of Preservationist attitudes. They are called here Twentieth-century Restoration and Vieux Carré Revival and are illustrated overleaf.

MH23 McDonogh 15 School, 721 St. Philip Street, 1931, E.A. Christy, architect; H. Pratt Farnsworth, contractor

MH23 *To the typical block form of the 1930s school building, architect Christy added a collection of details from older French Quarter buildings—round-headed windows with curving muntins, box balconies, plaster banding suggestive of pilasters and entablatures, a parapet with open tile work.*

VIEUX CARRÉ REVIVAL
DATES: 1920S TO THE PRESENT

The Vieux Carré Revival style is a twentieth-century mode characterized by copying pieces of earlier French Quarter buildings and combining them in new structures. Designers work within some style or combination of styles represented in the Quarter's historic inventory. The practice arises from a feeling that new construction should be essentially scenographic and that it should fill in gaps in the French Quarter fabric as inconspicuously as possible, leaving the limelight for older buildings. It is distrustful of more easily identifiable twentieth-century styles, including the various faces of Modernism. At its worst it has inspired a pronounced mediocrity, a search for the least common stylistic denominator from eclectic sources, constructed with the cheapest modern methods. Bernard Lemann noted the phenomenon in the 1960s and wrote, "ignorant or cost-cutting approximation of a flaccid historicism is in no way preferable to any other kind of rampant destructiveness." Many times this approach has yielded a "French Quarter look" little better than the ordinary suburban houses which have been supplied with unoccupiable balconies and marketed as "New Orleans style."[4]

At other times, however, in striking contrast to such cheap and exploitative examples, some admirable work has been done in this style. Richard Koch and E. A. Christy made interesting designs in this mode years before the Vieux Carré Commission was established. The best of this work, like similarly eclectic work done on public buildings and carefully crafted residences across America, deserves respect for its inventiveness and skill and for the genuine desire for contextual harmony it represents.

LL44A Le Petit Théâtre complex, entrance, before addition of second level

LL7 Le Petit Théâtre complex, 600-618 St. Peter Street; Orue-Pontalba reconstruction (at corner) 1962-63, Koch and Wilson; other theatre buildings, 1922, Armstrong and Koch, with later additions

LL7, LL44A *Le Petit Théâtre occupies what is designed to look like several structures. Perhaps the entrance above simulates an opening in a courtyard wall, though a second story was added later. The corner building is a reconstruction of the Orue-Pontalba house (p. 121). The controversial demolition and replacement of the venerable eighteenth-century building was argued on structural grounds. Balcony rails, doors, windows and woodwork were reused.*

MH18 *Taking cues from the Pedesclaux-Le Monnier house (p. 38), this hotel achieves a quiet, reasonably-scaled presence on the street. It has a successful courtyard.*

MH17 *An example was needed to show the depths of scaleless and ill-conceived construction possible within the twentieth-century Vieux Carré Revival style. This one suffices. It occupies the site of the French Opera House (p. 129) from which it learned nothing.*

MH19 *A granite arcade from the old St. Louis Hotel was incorporated into the side façade of the twentieth-century hotel which occupies its site. The gesture is an honest one, suggesting by the fragment the scale and nature of what has been replaced.*

MH18 718-30 Bienville Street, c. 1970, Richard Caldwell, architect

MH17 541 Bourbon Street, 1965

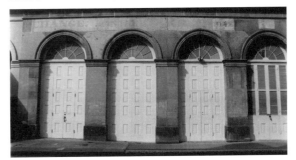

MH19 501 Chartres Street, originally built 1840, J.N.B. and J.I. de Pouilly, architects; reconstructed 1960, Curtis and Davis, architects, Koch and Wilson, associated architects

139

CL11 720-22 Toulouse Street, c. 1790, shown before restoration,

MH30 720-22 Toulouse Street, after restoration

CL11, MH30 *The Historic New Orleans Collection restored this Spanish Colonial structure to its early appearance, as shown in an archival drawing.*

L2 *In his restoration of Madame John's Legacy, architect Monroe Labouisse went to great lengths to retain original material. When portions of the rear railings near the posts were found rotten, those portions only were replaced and carefully joined to the sound remaining sections.*

BB2 *After a 1988 fire, the trusswork of the Cabildo was completely reconstructed as part of a restoration project. Concern for authenticity controlled each aspect of the work, from the selection of the wood to finding joiners skilled in historic techniques.*

AK47 *The restoration of the U.S. Mint emphasizes its structure and exposes the ductwork necessary to make it a functioning museum. Both the integrity of the original building and the fact of its restoration are evident to the visitor.*

L2 Madame John's Legacy, 628-32 Dumaine Street, 1788; restored 1972-73, Monroe Labouisse

TWENTIETH-CENTURY RESTORATION

DATES: 1960S TO THE PRESENT

Some of the most painstaking architectural work done in the Quarter in the twentieth century has been restoration work, the name we give to a serious attempt to take a building back to its appearance at either the time of its construction or at some selected moment in its history. Such work requires careful research and the re-enactment or simulation of historic construction practices. It also requires ingenuity in the inconspicuous insertion of the twentieth-century technology necessary for the building's new uses. Its techniques are most commonly used on museum structures, making the buildings themselves into historic artifacts for visitors' inspection.

BB2 Cabildo, Jackson Square, 1795-99, Gilberto Guillemard; restored 1994, Koch and Wilson, Architects, Robert J. Cangelosi, Jr., project architect

AK47 U.S. Mint, 400 Esplanade Avenue, 1835, William Strickland; restored 1979, E. Eean McNaughton, Architects; Biery and Toups, Architects; Bernard Lemann, consultant

MODERNISM
A LAMENT AND A MODEST PRESCRIPTION

Modernism is conspicuous by its absence from the French Quarter. Although the official position of the Vieux Carré Commission has been that good modern design should not be discouraged in new construction, in practice a stifling conservatism has prevailed. The architectural profession has done little to question the status quo. The result is that this district, remarkable for its catalog of styles going forward from the Ursuline Convent of 1750 to the early twentieth century, has been frozen through most of the present century, its vitality toned down and repressed, its catalog missing good examples of Modern work as surely as it misses the buildings destroyed in the conflagrations of 1788 and 1794. The twentieth century will be remembered as the period of Preservation in the Quarter. In the simplistic but prevalent view, Preservation and Modernism are incompatible opposites. The twentieth century is thought of as the age of destruction, and Modernism combines in people's minds with the destruction of nineteenth-century fabric. It is ironic, on the one hand, how flagrantly this flies in the face of the contextual preoccupations of late-Modernist architects for the last third of this century. It is equally ironic, on the other, that these preoccupations of architects have not produced an architecture humane enough to gain acceptance outside the congoscenti.

A prescription: what is needed in the Quarter are some new small-scaled infill projects of an experimental nature. They would be designed strictly to adhere to mixed-use zoning and to the Zoning Ordinance's current height, area and bulk requirements. But they would be allowed freedom in materials and façade design. Such projects have enlivened

MH74 534-36 Bienville Street, date uncertain, c. 1930?

Philadelphia's Society Hill for the past thirty years; Europe's cities are full of good examples. The French Quarter's buildings survived initially because New Orleans' traditional pace of change, not without its touch of lethargy, left the area alone. When that was not enough, energetic preservation efforts mobilized political and economic resources to hold onto as much of the building stock as possible. A remarkable amount has been accomplished. Much of great value has been saved. This saving must continue, but must be recognized as essentially a police action. The act of policing contains within it no vision for the future. Planning has been left to politics and economics, or to put it more plainly to politicians and developers, few of whom have understood the importance of what they are dealing with. The vitality of the preservation movement needs constant reinvigoration lest lethargy and its innately defensive posture overcome it. *An infusion of twentieth and twenty-first-century design, limited in scale and use but not in style, and especially not in quality, would help to sustain the French Quarter as an alive-and-breathing community of buildings with an internal process of renewal to allay the threat of suffocation from its own history.*

MH73 534-36 Bienville Street

MH74, MH73 *Neither the date nor the architect of this fanciful twentieth-century structure is known. It is appropriate in scale without attempting to look like "a French Quarter building." Its vitality (and the quizzical trio sitting on their pedestals) would not have survived the kind of stylistic design review required of current projects in the Vieux Carré.*

THE LIMITS OF ARCHITECTURAL ANALYSIS

Ultimately, architectural analysis cannot describe the French Quarter's collection of buildings any more fully than an anatomy text describes a human being. Categories of type and style come after the fact of the buildings themselves, and New Orleans builders have been nothing if not eclectic and flexible; some buildings bridge between types and styles or innovate in ways that utterly resist categorization. So much the better. The structures' best qualities (as one suspects could have been said of their builders as well) lie more in their craft and ingenuity than in their learning. That the crazy juxtaposition of self-important three-story townhouses with low, modest, carefully-made Creole cottages should yield a magical neighborhood attests not so much to architectural sophistication as to an alchemy of careful building, weather, time and a history of thoughtful human habitation.

MW111 cottage, demolished, formerly at 1040 Chartres Street, believed to date from the Spanish Colonial period

A NOTE ON CONSTRUCTION

EARLY CONSTRUCTION

New Orleans' swampy site presented an immediate challenge to its early colonists, who used the traditional construction methods they brought with them to build as best they could. Recent excavations in the French Quarter by Earth Search, Inc., for the Historic New Orleans Collection have uncovered the remains of a 1730 barracks structure built of vertical boards resting on a sizable timber sill set less than three feet below ground.[1] Known in French as *poteaux sur sole,* the method, placing wood in contact with watery soil, normally resulted in a quickly deteriorating foundation (though water-saturated soil was credited for having actually preserved some remaining timbers found in the excavation). Above ground, early structures employed heavy timbers, probably mortised and tenoned together in all but the most temporary structures. The joinery and the steep hipped roofs are within the tradition of medieval France.

USES OF BRICK

Brick quickly replaced wood for foundations, and was used in the parish church of St. Louis in 1727. Specifications of a century later for the Mortuary Chapel describe what must have become current practice for substantial structures by its construction date of 1826—brick foundations two-feet deep and twenty-eight inches thick, resting on three-inch cypress boards set on cross members spaced five feet apart.[3]

Our town is very beautiful, well laid out and evenly built, as well as I can tell. The streets are wide and straight. The main street is a league long. The houses are well-built of timber and mortar. The tops of the houses are covered with shingles, which are little planks, sharpened in the form of slates—one must see them to believe it—for this roofing has all the appearance and beauty of slate. There is a popular song sung here which says that this city is as beautiful as Paris. However, I find a difference between this city and Paris.

from a letter of Sister Madeleine Hachard, a young Ursuline nun, to her father in France, dated April 24, 1728[2]

LL4 Mortuary Chapel, now Our Lady of Guadalupe Chapel, 411 N. Rampart Street, 1826, Gurlie and Guillot

MW111 *Brick, stucco, wood and tile—common materials and straightforward construction characterize the traditional process of French Quarter building.*

LL4 *Our Lady of Guadalupe Chapel is near St. Louis Cemetery No. 1, which is just outside the French Quarter on Basin Street. Built as a mortuary chapel, it accommodated funerals when fear of contagion from yellow fever drove them out of the main church at Jackson Square. It is the city's oldest surviving church structure.*

145

A NOTE ON CONSTRUCTION

M30 Thierry house, after restoration

M30, M31 *A 1940 renovation uncovered Greek Doric columns within an enclosed gallery at the Thierry house. An early instance of interest in Greek architecture, the columns and segmental arches had been made of brick and plastered over. Portions of the moldings remained to guide their restoration by Koch and Wilson, Architects.[4]*

K208 *The construction of this narrow structure shows clearly after a fire. The walls were brick between posts. The roof structure consisted of light rafters, horizontally braced and sheathed with boards.*

M31 Thierry house after discovery of columns, 721 Gov. Nicholls Street, 1814, Arsène Lacarrière Latour and Henry Boneval Latrobe

K208 619 St. Philip Street, after fire, date uncertain

The Quarter's oldest surviving structure, the Ursuline Convent of 1750 (1100 Chartres Street), is built of solid brick, plastered over. For the most part, however, the use of solid masonry was not so successful in colonial times. Local clays produced soft bricks which had to be covered in either plaster or wood sheathing. The use of "lake brick" baked from superior clays found north of Lake Pontchartrain, gradually improved this situation. But the practice of protecting brick with plaster or wood sheathing continued for the most part until American influence in the nineteenth century fashioned a trend toward exposed red brick, referred to as "Northern brick" and often imported from East Coast cities such as Philadelphia and Baltimore. Such brick laid in a Flemish bond is evident on the façade of 1014 St. Louis Street (p. 44), built in 1831; at the sides it dovetails into less expensive material. The Hermann-Grima house (pp.47, 125), an elegant free-standing building of the same date, shows an example of another common practice of the time—narrow joints painted on the already-painted surface of its brickwork. (Actually, in the case of this house the brick underneath is Philadelphia brick laid in Flemish bond;[5] since the brick had been painted long ago, this "pencilling" method was used in its restoration.)

BRICK BETWEEN POSTS

Brick-between-posts, a combination of half-timber construction with brick infill, was a widespread practice from early colonial times, persisting into the mid-nineteenth century. The half-timbering derives from European practice. In Louisiana it provided a sound frame which was filled with soft local brick. Madame John's Legacy, a surviving house built in 1788 but believed to demonstrate construction practices from decades earlier, employs brick-between-posts (sheathed in wood) for its upper level and solid masonry (plastered) below (pp. 18-20). Such a combination would lift the timbers above the problem of constant wetness.

USES OF WOOD

Wood, of course, has been the abundant building material for a town situated among ancient cypress forests. From one viewpoint the city of New Orleans represents simply the conversion of these trees into the posts, lintels, beams, joists, studs, trusses, rafters, and purlins of the city's buildings. Many structures were made entirely of cypress, strong and rot-resistant, and the rest used it for floor and roof structure, flooring and millwork. Today "old cypress" is sought for re-use in renovations and new construction. In investigating damage to old structures one often finds the original material sound, the wood from more recent repairs deteriorated.

ELEVATION OF STRUCTURES

Except in the most primitive structures, floors were raised above the ground. (The higher elevation of modern streets and sidewalks often diminishes the height apparent at the street.) As levees brought flooding more nearly under control, houses raised to the level of Madame John's Legacy became rare. But buildings grew at the top; the fear that structures over two stories would sink into the mire was overcome with the Pedesclaux-Le Monnier house, completed 1811 (p. 38). It is the third floor that set this house apart as structually daring. (The fourth floor is presumed to be an addition.) Its bravado is shown by the fact that it exceeds the two-story height of the Cabildo and the Presbytère on Jackson Square, roughly contemporary *public* buildings. Within a few decades the tall-ceilinged brick three-and-a-half-story American townhouses were commonplace, often sitting among lower cottages to shape the Quarter's active roofscape.

M2A Lafitte's Blacksmith Shop, 939-41 Bourbon Street, probably after 1781

B1 726-28 Toulouse Street, c. 1830

M2A *The brick-between-posts construction of this Bourbon Street cottage is evident because of the missing stucco. Although some early builders attempted to expose the structure, the results were not successful. The soft local bricks required the protection of stucco or weatherboards (and still do).*

B1 *A substantial truss of morticed and pegged members extends along the roof ridge of this Creole cottage. An unusual condition, it has been exposed in a recent renovation of the cottage by the Historic New Orleans Collection. Architects Peter Trapolin and Daniel Samuels devised a double roof structure to allow the space to be insulated at the same time the truss and sheathing boards are exposed.*

147

A NOTE ON CONSTRUCTION

MH31 pan tile cottage roof, 823-25 Bourbon Street, c. 1830

MH31 *The pan tile roof of this Creole cottage is one of the few that survives in the French Quarter. Such a roof of flat tiles would have been common in the eighteenth and nineteenth centuries.*

MH58 attic of service structure, 823-25 Bourbon Street

MH58, MH57 *Trusses support the roof of the service structure. Lath is laid, spaced apart, across the rafters. Each tile has a "hook", an extension of the tile, which allows it to hang from the lath. The tiles and their hooks are evident in the photograph. The system is sufficiently loose to allow a measure of ventilation for the attic.*

MH57 roof construction of service structure, 823-25 Bourbon Street

ROOFS

Hovering hipped roofs are the most characteristic of French Quarter building tops, if not the most common. The ones with double pitches comprise a remarkably clear structural diagram of their origins. Rafters of shallow pitch, often cantilevered over a sidewalk or supported on the posts of a gallery, intersect with the steeper part, usually a timber truss bearing on a solid exterior wall. Such triangular trusses as those in the steep parts are described in old building documents as "French", showing their origins as plainly as the floating shallow parts recall the porch-sheltered dwellings of the Caribbean. The comparison made on p. 19 of the Ursuline Convent with Madame John's Legacy of forty years later shows this relationship as an evolution, undoubtedly brought about by the need to shelter such walls and windows as the Convent's from intense sun and rain.[6] Otherwise, the construction of the Quarter's variety of hipped and gabled roofs seems unremarkable. Their handsome timber joinery, often impressive for the material and for the skill it represents, are rarely exposed in habitable spaces except in twentieth-century renovations.

Trees provided the actual roofing as well as the structure for the earliest buildings, their wood split into shingles or, more primitively, their bark laid over a wooden frame. Tile was used early in the French Colonial period and continued in use well into the nineteenth century, still surviving in a few rare cases such as the Napoleon House (500 Chartres Street) and the Creole cottage at 823-25 Bourbon Street.

Such steep roofs used flat tiles formed with a protrusion for hooking them onto spaced strips of wood running perpendicular to the rafters. Barrel tiles, so called for their rounded shape, were used for shallower slopes. Flat tiles were also used for "terrace roofs", the nearly flat roofs popular for several decades around 1800. Sally Reeves describes their installation "over a course of bricks covered with sheathing paper and then pitch and tar."[7] Tile continued to be a common roofing material in the nineteenth century, gradually replaced by slate.

Builders from France, Canada, the Caribbean, and Spain responded to New Orleans' damp, warm climate and high water table with generally conservative solutions—traditional frame and masonry construction, the two put together in various combinations. The fine points of French Quarter construction, and even some more obvious matters, have not received a great deal of attention from architects or historians. Many telling relationships between construction practices in New Orleans and the building traditions from which they come remain to be explored.

AK1 roofscape

AK1 *Roofs of French Quarter buildings are simple combinations of hipped, shed and gabled forms. From above, their clear shapes make a terrain of their own, more varied than the flat one on which their structural loads rest.*

B3 *Mortised and pegged truss work furnishes an attic space in the Historic New Orleans Collection. Its shapes suggest the trees from which it was made*

B3 attic of the Merieult house (now the Historic New Orleans Collection), 527-33 Royal Street, 1792, Jacob Copperwaite, builder

149

THREATS TO THE FRENCH QUARTER

K124 address uncertain

What of the French Quarter today? One feels obliged, if nervous, to leave the architect's view for a moment and comment on wider forces at work.

The forces are not necessarily benign. A volume of tourists undreamt of fifty years ago, along with rising property values and speculative opportunities, have actually decreased the resident population of the Quarter. While some buildings are almost excessively preserved, a surprising number stand empty. Too many upper stories are not used—whole buildings are blighted by exploitative ground-floor usage which renders the upper levels ravaged by noise and other inhospitable influences. When a t-shirt shop or an entertainment operation pays enormous rent for a ground floor, a landlord may forget the residential upper floors of his building. Inflexible building codes, designed for new construction, conflict with the eccentricity and fragility of these structures. Several prime blocks near the River, presently used for surface parking, are ripe for redevelopment, for which no thoughtful plan has been officially put forward.

The vast majority of Quarter structures are not replaceable in any reasonable way. Maintaining the integrity of the French Quarter means more than regulating external changes to individual buildings. The District's needs go beyond façade design and questions of style, the principal concerns of the Vieux Carré Commission's design review. The doors and windows and stairs and mantels, the loggias that mediate between inside and out, the courtyards and other open spaces (protected in theory by zoning, but not always in practice)—must be understood as integral to these buildings. Change will happen, as it always has. But change should pass through the complex filter of appropriateness, to the individual building and to the district as a whole.

Who is to solve these problems? Optimistic activists, more than philosphers, are responsible for the French Quarter's being with us still. If New Orleans' mood of *laissez faire* kept things from being destroyed in the past, crusaders, both local and imported, have played a bigger part in this century. Their work is cut out for them.

Fundamental to preserving the community of buildings is the maintenance of a civilized environment for those who live and work in the Quarter, because the buildings and courtyards especially, but also the streets and parks, require the care of concerned residents. The residents are a beleaguered lot, crowded by tourists and traffic, threatened by street criminals, tempted to profit from the very spiral of rising tourist densities and property values that threaten their world. But they are the life blood of the Quarter, and they know it. Those who stand up to the challenge, buttressed by their supporters in city government and the Vieux Carré Commission, are the real heroes of the current scene. For their trouble they have one of the nation's richest urban environments for their neighborhood.

A couple of ideas might be helpful.

1. *Concentrate some of the city's supply of intelligence and talent on solving the Quarter's problems by scrutinizing it both internally and in relation to the whole city. The major internal problems must be addressed: abused buildings; parking; open space; security. The process of planning in New Orleans has tended to be reactive, often constrained by politicians out to preserve their patronage rather than their city. The situation is too critical for that.*

Once any group of astute people looks at the larger picture, one solution becomes obvious:

2. *Reduce the density of tourists in the French Quarter and help other struggling neighbor-*

hoods at the same time. New Orleans still has a phenomenal stock of nineteenth century buildings outside the Quarter, many in largely intact neighborhoods which cry for attention and renewal. Would it not make sense to spread the tourists out by offering more streetcars with more destinations, helping neighborhood restaurants and other enterprises, and reducing the pressure on the Quarter?

The Cathedral bells sound different, even new sometimes, depending on the weather and one's mood. Like their sound, the District has the power to sustain and renew itself and the city's collective view of it—our particular generation's take on the French Quarter myth. Maintaining the myth has been part of the role of the preservation movement, active since the 1920s and imbued with legal clout since the 1930s. The Quarter we see today would be a far different place, both physically and psychologically, had the preservation movement not occurred.

It is necessary to realize, however, that what we call "preservation" never literally preserves the past. The world changes around us as we try to preserve it, and the very efforts of preservationists change the thing "preserved." Struggles at preservation simply affect the nature of change— selecting what parts of things to hold onto and deciding how to change the rest. To do it well, one's ends must be clearly in mind.

The goal is a healthy, continually evolving community. Its health will be manifest in well-used buildings which are respected and tended by the people who inhabit them. Fostering the symbiosis between these structures and their inhabitants is the key to sustaining the French Quarter as a living community, the thing it has been since 1718. To do less would be a tragedy.

MW4 Louisiana State Bank building, 401-03 Royal Street, designed 1820, completed 1822, Benjamin Henry Latrobe, architect; Benjamin Fox, builder

MW4 *The rear wall of Latrobe's bank swells into a courtyard in a stylistic gesture typical of its time (think of the south front of the White House). The Morgan Whitney photograph shows a courtyard which is open as it needs to be, instead of the enclosed condition which suffocates the rear of this building today.*

Each of us knows a different French Quarter.

This book puts forth a rational organization of the things French Quarter buildings have in common—a set of types, styles, components, construction methods, the layout of buildings within streets and blocks, and a fragment of history equal to their years of survival. The problem with rational methods of organization, however, is that we let them stand in place of the thing being organized. Having grasped the notion of building types, we think we have grasped the buildings themselves, and of course we have not. Any organization of these buildings can only be meaningful if the buildings are known in other ways first, or at least at the same time.

To that end, the photographs provide another way of knowing them.

A photograph is limited to one place and one moment, and, like Cable's story about Madame John's Legacy, it can add its own particular way of seeing to an already familiar place. Many of the photographs used in this book are old ones taken at various moments in previous decades of this century, and some are still older. They exemplify the layered nature of change and continuity in the Quarter. Some of them show scenes of a quietness nearly impossible today. Others freeze moments when buildings fronts were painted signs, when a different generation of automobiles lined the streets, when buildings which are now derelict were maintained, when buildings which are now pristine were derelict. We can learn from these moments what we've gained and what we've lost. We can learn from these photographs an appreciation not only for buildings but also for attitudes which have allowed buildings to be clearly seen and thoughtfully

cared for. The old photographs shown here are the work of local photographers who add their individual frames to the city's collective cinema of itself.

The photographs come from a variety of sources, but the largest single source is the Southeastern Architectural Archive of Tulane University. The Archive is an extraordinary repository of photographs as well as of architectural drawings, models, and artifacts. Within the Archive are a number of collections of photographs. Photographs from the Archive in this book are identified by a code indicating the collection from which they come. When a collection contains the work of more than one photographer, the identity of the photographer is individually given below.

Copyrights of all photographs used from the Southeastern Architectural Archive are controlled by the Archive. Three photographs from the Historic New Orleans Collection are under copyright by the Collection which also exercises separate control over the Clarence Laughlin photographs. In all other cases, copyrights are controlled by the individual photographers. No further reproduction of these photographs can be made without permission.

The small captions under each picture are provided to make the photographs useful as documentation. They give the name, if any, by which a building has been locally known; its street address; and its date of construction (usually from the Vieux Carré Survey). If available, the person responsible for design and/or construction, again usually from the Survey, is listed. Distinctions between architect and builder were not clear for most of these buildings; that distinction is made only when it seems justified by information in the Survey or elsewhere.

153

CREDITS FOR PHOTOGRAPHS & DRAWINGS

Effort was made to verify the locations of photographs. Some of the archival photographs had addresses, some did not; some were incorrect; some were more subject to checking than others. If errors remain in spite of the care taken, apologies are duly offered. Also, the decision was made that uncertainty of address should not preclude use of photos, so some are listed without addresses. Dates of construction and architect or builder information is omitted in the Components section because it would have implied the date or designer of the component itself, which is not necessarily that of the building. With archival photographs, there is always the possibility that conditions shown in the photographs no longer exist. This is useful for recording purposes and restoration work but possibly frustrating for the searcher. When structures are known to have been demolished, they are so noted.

The phototgraphs vary in quality because they were made for different purposes. Some, like those of Morgan Whitney, show studied compositions, so care was taken not to crop them. Some, like the Clarence Laughlin photographs, are beautifully printed. Others were simple contact prints made mainly for documentary purposes. These were cropped when it enhanced their usefulness. An image that has received more than minimal cropping is usually labeled "detail." In most cases care has been taken to show the images as they were found in the Archive; technological "doctoring" has been avoided.

Maps and ironwork drawings were made for this book and are covered by its copyright. For consistency of style, architectural drawings were redrawn from a variety of sources, especially the Historic American Buildings Survey. These redrawings are also covered by the copyright of the book. Because of their exceptional draftsmanship, drawings for the "Miscellaneous Hardware" section were scanned directly from prints of the Historic American Buildings Survey drawings.

The following is an alphabetical listing of prefixes, together with whatever additional information is necessary to identify the photographer of each photograph and the artist of each drawing. Dates or approximate dates of photographs and drawings are indicated where known.

AK   Alan Karchmer; photographs; c. 1980.

ARH   Alicia Rogan Heard; maps, fortifications, and ironwork drawings; 1996 and 1997.

B   Jan White Brantley, photographer; Historic New Orleans Collection, 1990-1996

BB   Robert S. Brantley and Jan White Brantley, photographers; 1993.

CL   Clarence J. Laughlin Collection, Southeastern Architectural Archive; Clarence J. Laughlin, photographer (1905-1985); dates of photographs range from the 1930s to the 1950s. *Special note:* The Historic New Orleans Collection purchased copyright to Clarence Laughlin's photographs in 1981 and exercises control over their use.

HABS   Historic American Buildings Survey; drawings; delineators and dates of drawings:
HABS.2 delineator, B. Proctor, 1934
HABS.4 delineator, R.G. Foster, 1934
HABS.6-HABS.9 delineators, Cecil R. Coleman, Alvyk Boyd Cruise; 1940

HC Howard "Cole" Coleman Collection, Southeastern Architectural Archive; Howard "Cole" Coleman, photographer (1883-1969); photographs date from the 1960s.

K Walter Cook Keenan Collection, Southeastern Architectural Archive; Walter Cook Keenan, photographer (1881-1970); photographs range in date from c. 1945-1952.

L Monroe Labouisse; photographs made from his own slides of Madame John's Legacy after its restoration, for which he was the architect; c. 1973. Courtesy of Waggonner and Ball, Architects. L5 is from the same collection but the slide was labeled "old photograph."

LL Louisiana Landmarks Society Collection, Southeastern Architectural Archive; photographs from a range of unidentified sources and dates.

M Southeastern Architectural Archive, miscellaneous collections. M10 view of Madame John's Legacy is from *Artwork of New Orleans*, Chicago, the W.H. Parish Pub. Co., 1895. M29 Ernest J. Bellocq, photographer (1883-1949)

MH Malcolm Heard, photographer; photographs date from 1996-1997.

MW Morgan Whitney Collection, Southeastern Architectural Archive, gift of Mrs. Arthur F. Morris; Morgan Whitney, photographer (1869-1913); dates of photographs range from c. 1890 to 1906.

RA Rebecca Anderson; drawings; 1996-97.

RH Rudolf Hertzberg Collection; Southeastern Architectural Archive; Rudolf Hertzberg, photographer; date of photographs, c. 1937.

RK Richard Koch Collection, Southeastern Architectural Archive; contact prints; Richard Koch, photographer (1889-1971); dates of photographs range from the 1930s to the 1960s.

RKm Richard Koch Collection, Southeastern Architectural Archive; mounted contact prints; Richard Koch, photographer (1889-1971); dates of photographs range from the 1930s to the 1960s.

RT Ray Thompson Collection, Southeastern Architectural Archive; photographs by several photographers, including the following:
RT4 Louis T. Fritch
RT5-RT8 Frances B. Johnston (c. 1864-1952), photographs date from the 1930s
RT9-RT10 Leon Trice
RT11, RT14-RT15 Wood Whitesell

NOTES

Introduction: The Grid on the River

1. Records of the American Catholic Historical Society of Philadelphia, June 1899, pp. 201-207, cited by Samuel Wilson, Jr., *The Vieux Carre, New Orleans, Its Plan, Its Growth, Its Architecture* (New Orleans, 1968), p. 4.

2. Cultural geographer Peirce Lewis explored the city as a product of its geography in his ingenious book, *New Orleans, The Making of an Urban Landscape* (Cambridge, Massachusetts, 1976).

3. John Chase, *Frenchmen, Desire, Good Children, And Other Streets of New Orleans*, Second Edition (New Orleans, 1960).

4. Wilson, *Vieux Carre*, pp. 57-59.

5. Robert C. Reinders, *End of an Era, New Orleans, 1850-1860* (New Orleans, 1964), p. 5.

6. Reinders, pp. 5-7.

7. Map by Joseph Pilié, 1818, New Orleans Public Library, reproduced in Wilson, *Vieux Carre*, pp. 68-69. French Quarter as shown in *Robinson's Atlas*, 1883, reproduced in Wilson, *Vieux Carre*, p. 95.

8. Richard O. Baumbach, and William E. Borah, *The Second Battle of New Orleans, A History of the Vieux Carré Riverfront-Expressway Controversy* (University, Alabama, 1981).
This book recounted the complete history of the expressway proposal and its ultimate defeat.

I Types of French Quarter Houses

1. Samuel Wilson, Jr., "'Madame John's Legacy'—The Manuel Lanzos House," *The Architecture of Colonial Louisiana*, Jean M. Farnsworth and Ann M. Masson, editors (Lafayette, Louisiana, 1987), p. 336.

2. Capt. Philip Pittman, *The Present State of the European Settlements on the Mississippi* (London 1770; Cleveland 1906), pp. 42-43, as cited in Wilson, *Vieux Carré* , p. 102.

3. Reinders, *End of an Era*, p. 5.

4. Benjamin Henry Latrobe, *Impressions Respecting New Orleans, Diary and Sketches, 1818-1820*, edited with an introduction and notes by Samuel Wilson, Jr. (New York: 1951), pp. 105-106.

5. George Washington Cable, "Madame Delphine," *Old Creole Days* (Norwalk, Connecticut: 1971; original publication, 1879), p. 94.

6. Cable, "Café des Exilés," *Old Creole Days*, p. 188.

7. Lafcadio Hearn, "The Scenes of Cable's Romances," reprinted in *Old Creole Days*, p. xxvii.

8. Wilson, *Vieux Carré*, p. 109.

9. Jay D. Edwards, *Louisiana's Remarkable French Vernacular Architecture* (Baton Rouge,1988), p. 22.

10. Sally K. Reeves, "Correjolles and Chaigneau, *Entrepreneurs de Bâtiments* of Creole New Orleans," *Preservation in Print*, publication of the Preservation Resource Center of New Orleans, February 1996 (pp. 10 ff.) and March 1996, (pp. 16 ff.).

11. Latrobe, *Impressions*, p. 42.

12. John Michael Vlach, "The Shotgun House: An African Architectural Legacy," *Common Places, Readings in American Vernacular Architecture*, edited by Dell Upton and John Michael Vlach (Athens, Georgia, and London, 1986).

13. Latrobe, *Impressions*, pp. 105-106.

14. Lafcadio Hearn, *Creole Sketches* (Boston, 1924), p. 181. Hearn wrote these pieces for the New Orleans *Item* between 1878 and 1881. He lived in New Orleans for ten years, beginning in 1877.

II Components of French Quarter Buildings

1. Harriet Martineau, "The Haunted House," in *The World from Jackson Square,* edited by Etolia S. Basso (New York, 1948), p. 122.

2. Edwards, *Louisiana's French Vernacular Architecture,* pp. 6-8.

3. Latrobe, *Impressions,* p. 87.

4. Marcus Christian, *Negro Ironworkers of Louisiana, 1718-1900,* (New Orleans, 1972), *passim.*

5. Ann M. Masson and Lydia J. Owen, "Cast Iron and the Crescent City," catalog for an exhibition at Gallier House, New Orleans,1975-1976, p. 13.

6. Hearn, *"A Creole Courtyard"* from *Creole Sketches,* pp. 78-81, this sketch originally published in the New Orleans *Item,* November 11, 1879.

7. Edwards, *Louisiana's French Vernacular Architecture,* p. 8.

III An Illustrated Glossary of Styles

1. Samuel Wilson, Jr., and Leonard V. Huber, *The Cabildo on Jackson Square* (New Orleans, 1973), p. 65.

2. Leonard V. Huber and Samuel Wilson, Jr., *Baroness Pontalba's Buildings* (New Orleans, 1964) p. 30.

3. Legislation established as a matter of state and local law the preservation of "the quaint and distinctive character" of the French Quarter. The Vieux Carré Commission, which has an appointed Commission and a paid Director and staff, began operation in 1936. Having weathered numerous tempests of state, local and neighborhood politics, the Commission survives today with offices in the old Bank of Louisiana building above the police station at 334 Royal Street. It controls changes to the exterior of all structures within its district.

4. Bernard Lemann, *The Vieux Carré, A General Statement* (New Orleans, 1966), p. 77.

A Note on Construction

1. Jon Kukla, "Eureka! Uncovering the Great Fire of 1788 and a Royal Barracks from the 1730s" in *The Historic New Orleans Collection Newsletter,* vol. IX, no. 4, Fall 1991, pp. 1-4.

2. "The Letters of Sister Madeleine Hachard de Saint-Stanislas" from Basso, editor, *The World from Jackson Square,* p. 40.

3. Specifications of Gurlie and Guillot for the Mortuary Chapel, quoted in Samuel Wilson, Jr., "The Mortuary Chapel, New Orleans, Louisiana," *The Louisiana Architect,* May 1969.

4. *Conversations with Samuel Wilson, Jr., Dean of Architectural Preservation in New Orleans,* compiled and edited by Abbye A. Gorin (New Orleans, 1991), pp. 34-35.

5. Wilson, *Vieux Carré,* p. 113.

6. Jay D. Edwards classified the roof shapes of galleried Louisiana vernacular structures in *Louisiana's French Vernacular Architecture,* p. 4.

7. Reeves, "Correjolles and Chaigneau" in *Preservation in Print,* March 1996, p. 17.

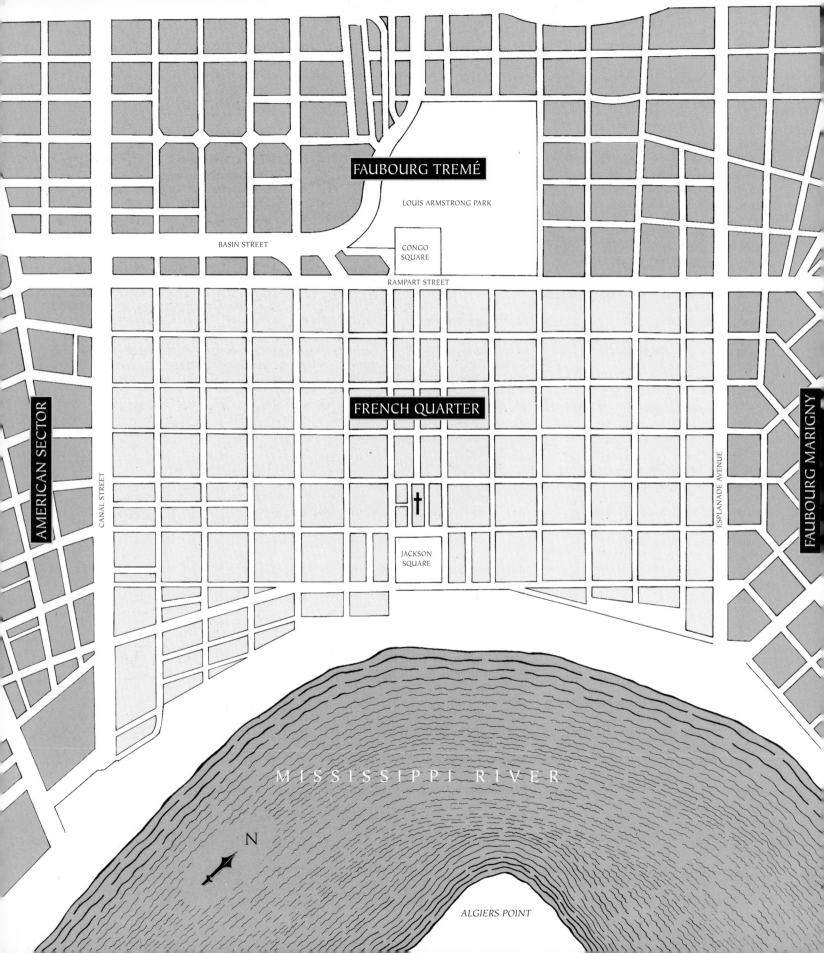

FAUBOURG TREMÉ

LOUIS ARMSTRONG PARK

CONGO
SQUARE

BASIN STREET

RAMPART STREET

FRENCH QUARTER

AMERICAN SECTOR

CANAL STREET

ESPLANADE AVENUE

FAUBOURG MARIGNY

JACKSON
SQUARE

MISSISSIPPI RIVER

N

ALGIERS POINT